This is a profound book about a simple idea: that the secret of being human is God's gracious love to us and our response of love to him and others. Compelling stories and practical advice build on theological insight and sociological reflection, all served up with a dash of humour. The result is a book that will inspire you, and then help you, to love well and therefore live well.

TIM CHESTER
Pastor of Grace Church Boroughbridge; Faculty Member of Crosslands Training; Author

Mark Greene is a legend. When I grow up I'd like to be more like him. I can always trust Mark to have his finger on the pulse of God and the world. I can't think of a better opportunity than this book to learn the deep and beautiful Christian foundation essential for our times – Love.

DANIELLE STRICKLAND
Speaker, Author and Social Justice Advocate

Detaching relationships from banking leads to a global crash. Detaching relationships from sex leads to hurt and pain. Detaching relationships from politics leads to ugly tribalism. In this book, Mark Greene brilliantly shows that loving relationships should be central to a healthy world because they are central to its wonderful Creator, who is Three-in-One.

ANDY FLANNAGAN
Executive Director, Christians in Politics

Full of grace, wisdom and hope, Mark explores the transformational power of a distinctive relational lens for every sphere of life. When, as organizations, communities and individuals, our daily purpose is to love, value and respect other people, we weave a pattern of life that goes with the grain of the universe.

DR. SHIRLEY JENNER
Lecturer, Global Development Institute, University of Manchester

To the Christian, this book may be thought to state the 'Basil Fawlty' obvious. Jesus told us in clear terms what are the two most important things in life. But working that out in reality is the issue, isn't it? With real life examples and Mark's chutzpah sense of humour, any reader will get the five main principles involved in putting Jesus' saying into practice in all the different areas of life. Mark makes clear that there is no tension, logical or practical, in fulfilling our calling to love our neighbour and improve their lot whilst presenting the good news of Jesus' life-changing offer, however limited our energy. Nor is there tension between our calling to love God and look for Jesus' return whilst doing all we can to improve the welfare of those around us. We are all apprentices of Jesus in this, and this book just may – probably will – inspire you and encourage you to put into practice what is not just probably the best idea in the world.

SIR JEREMY COOKE
International Arbitrator; Former High Court Judge

In this inspiring book, Mark Greene draws us into a compelling vision of a God who is inherently relational and utterly interested in the authenticity, generosity and practicality of our relationships. It offers great ideas for transforming everyday frontline contexts, helping us see them through the lens of the kind of love to which Jesus calls us, with very helpful, practical suggestions for workplaces, churches, marriages and parenthood. While our generation may well be the most connected in history, Mark's attractive vision of lived-out love for one's neighbour is more needed than ever, and this book highlights the unique opportunity the church has to model genuine community which leads to our human flourishing.

ANDY WOLFE
Dean of Younger Leadership College, Diocese of Southwell & Nottingham; Former Vice Principal, The Nottingham Emmanuel School

Mark Greene's simple message about the importance of good relationships has challenged me to reassess how I apply the greatest commandment in my interactions with people at home, work, in my community and more broadly. His great skills as a storyteller makes this book as accessible as it is profound. This is a must-read for anyone seeking to work out their faith wherever God puts them, but perhaps it should be a must-read too for our policy makers, and community and business leaders, as the prize is so great for us as a society if we learn (or relearn) to live more relationally.

JOËLLE WARREN MBE, DL
Executive Chair, Warren Partners

It has been a joy and privilege for us at the Jubilee Centre to be companions with Mark Greene and LICC along the road of discovering the depth and breadth of God's vision for true human flourishing – without question the Best Idea in the World. Mark's perceptive and imaginative writing teases out what this means, demonstrating powerfully that it's much more than an idea – it's a calling, a lifestyle, a vision and a purpose that can and should capture our heart and soul all life long!

JONATHAN TAME
Executive Director, Jubilee Centre

Inspiring, moving, practical, life-transforming. The principles of relational living in this book not only have profound implications for every area of life but have the power to transform the world of modern healthcare.

JOHN WYATT,
Emeritus Professor of Neonatal Paediatrics, University College London

(Probably) the best book I have read on this subject! I read *The R Factor* many moons ago, and still have a copy on my bookshelf. I am so pleased that Mark Greene has taken up the challenge to republish this excellent material in his own inimitable style. He encourages us with wit, humour and up-to-date real-life examples, to step beyond our self-obsessed culture – and to take seriously Jesus' command to love God and to love each other. Read it and you will be challenged to join the adventure of playing your part in creating a better world.

KATHARINE HILL
UK Director, Care for the Family

PROBABLY
THE BEST
IDEA IN
THE WORLD

Also by Mark Greene

Thank God it's Monday

Let My People Grow
(Mark Greene and Tracy Cotterell)

Pocket Prayers for Work

Of Love, Life and Caffè Latte

Fruitfulness on the Frontline

Adventure

PROBABLY THE BEST IDEA IN THE WORLD

MARK GREENE

Muddy
Pearl

First published in 2018 by
Muddy Pearl, Edinburgh, Scotland.
www.muddypearl.com
books@muddypearl.com

British Library Cataloguing in Publication Data
A catalogue record for this book is available from the British Library.

ISBN 978-1-910012-55-0

Cover Design by David McNeill
Typeset in Minion by David McNeill
www.revocreative.co.uk

Printed in Great Britain by Bell & Bain Ltd, Glasgow.

For the Trinamic Trio,
Anna-Marie, Tomi and Matt,
Knights of the Oblong Table, SPLY.

CONTENTS

A PAUSE FOR GRATITUDE

This little offering is about a simple but very big idea. As it happens, it's not my idea. It was Michael Schluter's idea. For years, I tried to cajole Michael (CBE) into writing a short version of the groundbreaking book, *The R Factor*, where he and David Lee introduced their thinking and primarily applied it to social policy. Michael, with the stubbornness of a cliff and the gentleness of a butterfly, consistently demurred. In the end, he asked me to write it. Then he started cajoling me. It took him rather less time to break me down, because I'd taught the material in myriad contexts and I'd seen its liberating impact on thousands of people, and I knew this wasn't some faddish novelty that would sparkle today and be gone tomorrow.

Many others have helped along the way, not least my colleagues at LICC (London Institute for Contemporary Christianity). In particular, I owe a great deal to Christina Winn, whose combination of perspicacity and personal engagement have been invaluable; to Stephanie Heald, whose selfless, thoughtful brilliance added yeast to the whole loaf; to Helen Valler, whose antennae for clarity are so highly tuned; to Team Zondervan, the original publisher, and now to Team Muddy Pearl – Stephanie, Anna, Healey, Fiona and Josh – whose careful and joyous way of working is a splendid example of this book's ideas in action.

Originally, of course, the understanding of the vital significance of this idea comes from the mind of Jesus, though, as experience has shown, you don't have to be one of his followers to reap some of its benefits, even if you will miss out on the greatest harvest. There is, after all, much, much more to the wisdom of Jesus than this big idea. Nevertheless, there are few that offer such a simple, rich, practical and integrated way forward in every aspect of life – Monday to Monday.

I hope you will be as grateful for it as I am.

Mark Greene

THE LONDON INSTITUTE
FOR CONTEMPORARY CHRISTIANITY
MARCH 2018

FOREWORD

If you want to see what's really important to people, go to a funeral and listen to the eulogy.

Rarely will a eulogy commemorate the deceased by recalling the size of the house in which they lived, or the salary they earned, or the kind of car they drove, or the holidays they enjoyed, or even (in most cases) the jobs they toiled at. Most of the things we spend most of the time chasing after are soon forgotten. Rather, eulogies tend to remember the deceased for three reasons: their creative qualities – she was a brilliant musician, a wonderful artist, a fine poet; their moral diligence – he was trustworthy, industrious, hard-working, conscientious; and, supremely, their relational nature – she was always there for me, a dad I could rely on, the best friend I could have hoped for.

I have long been struck how these qualities resonate with the question in Christian theology about what being made in the *imago dei* – the image of God – actually means. Drawing on the creation stories of Genesis 1–3, it is interpreted in rich ways. Being made in the image of God means we are created to be creative, productive and generous. It means we are created with a purpose, with work to do, creation to take care of. And it means we are created to relate to him, to other humans and to the rest of creation in a way that reflects something of God's own relational, Trinitarian nature.

Perhaps it is that at funerals, all the mess and busyness of life is swept aside, and we catch a glimpse of the horizon, or what we really, in our heart of hearts, in the light of eternity, aspire to be. We want to be remembered for how we created, how we loved, how we communicated, how we connected with one another.

Today we connect in innumerable ways. Indeed, in one sense, we are more connected than ever before. We tweet, we blog, we vlog, we skype, and we post till the cows come home and often till the larks rise. We cannot help but communicate. And yet it is increasingly clear that we are connected but not connecting. We may be richer, better educated, more comfortable than, say, our grandparents' generation, but we are no happier than they were, and in many instances we are more worried and more lonely.

How did this happen?

Some of it is due to the specific problems of the day. Young people today face a steeper, and more expensive climb into adulthood than they did twenty or forty years ago. The world is a less certain place. The West is no longer calling all the shots. Many of us have the spectre of a financial crash or terrorist atrocity hovering at the periphery of our vision. But there is also something deeper going on. The very thing that is (allegedly) behind modern progress – the freedom to live our lives exactly the way we choose – is also behind what is making us more miserable. Freedom is a wonderful thing – but when it is disembodied from the truth of human nature it can become as much a curse as a blessing.

This truth is in that *imago dei* and in the funeral eulogies: the truth that we are made for each other and for God. We are creative, responsible, *relational* beings, existing because of and for others, and the Other. We are persons slowly sculpted by love or eroded by the lack of it. Our freedom is a gift, from the God of Love, for the Love of God. I am only really me, if we are really us. That message of the freedom and joy to be found in loving others and loving God is at the heart of Jesus' teaching, his living and his death. It is at the heart of the Christian scriptures. And it makes intuitive sense: as soon as you start seeing the world through relational lenses, you understand it and are able to navigate it better.

I spent five enormously enjoyable, productive and beneficial years working at The London Institute for Contemporary Christianity and the Jubilee Centre, working with two people who really heard and lived that message, communicating it with rigour, intelligence, flair and warmth. Mark Greene and Michael Schluter are people worth listening to. Michael's wonderful idea of 'relational thinking' explained, expanded and richly applied by Mark with his customary verve, wit and joy is an idea worth pondering and living out. It is also what we need today, as we find ourselves with wealth that can sometimes feel impoverishing, and freedom that can sometimes feel imprisoning. It is, indeed, probably the best idea in the world.

Nick Spencer

DIRECTOR OF RESEARCH, THEOS

Author of *The Political Samaritan: How power hijacked a parable* (Bloomsbury, 2017) and *The Evolution of the West: How Christianity has shaped our values* (SPCK, 2016)

LONDON, MARCH 2018

Still the memory shimmers,
In the depth of our souls,
Of how close, how close
We all once were.
MARK GREENE

CHAPTER 1

THE BIG QUESTION

or

WHAT A DIFFERENCE A LENS MAKES

I was twenty-three at the time, young and eager in my first suit, working in advertising, with a spring in my step and a flower in my buttonhole. It was 1978, and wearing a flower in a buttonhole, except for weddings, had ceased to be any kind of convention at least 150 years before. Still, I rather liked it, and it distracted attention from the fact that I only had two suits in an era when suits were what you wore, and only having two was at least one too few for a man in an image-conscious business.

Michael Baulk was already a legend in the agency, slim and crisp in beautifully tailored light-hued suits, driving a sleek Ferrari and inspiring confidence in clients, hard work in subordinates and a good measure of awe from us new trainees. It was an awe only mildly tempered by our sense that, for some of our more senior colleagues, this man's determination and focus seemed a little too intense, a little too steely, merciless perhaps, to trust him with the agency's heart. Nevertheless, we knew that to be chosen to work for him would be like being recruited for MI6 – he emanated excellence.

Anyway, about three months into the job, we trainees were clucking away in a cubicle at the end of the day and 'he' appeared, still crisp and perfectly groomed in his beige and unrumpled suit, the creases of his trousers sharper than a surgeon's scalpel. And there in the disarray of that dark and tiny cubicle, far from the bright lights and wide open spaces of his office, he began to talk about advertising, about what it would take to succeed in this business and about the need for mentors to help us along the way. I was transfixed. It was as if the Pope had paused by my shed and was pouring out his wisdom. Who were we to merit such attention? Then Michael said this: 'The key to great advertising is strategic relevance and creative brilliance.'

There it was. In a nutshell.

We'd been to countless seminars, read piles of documents, talked to lots of people and visited every department in the agency, but here it was, five words that cut through to the very heart of the matter: 'strategic relevance and creative brilliance' – make sure you are saying the right thing, and then say it brilliantly. Of course, that doesn't make creating great advertising any easier. Strategic relevance takes hard work to fashion, and creative brilliance can't be conjured up by just adding an egg. Still, it immediately gave us two simple criteria to judge any work we did.

If only the rest of life were that simple.

Perhaps it can be.

Imagine someone asked you, 'What is the key to the good life?'

How would you reply? What is the one thing you would want to pass on to someone that would help them lead a fulfilling life? Of course, your answer might depend on who's asking and where you are at the time. After all, it's one thing to answer the question on the fifth floor of a chi-chi ad agency in an affluent Western democracy, it's quite another to answer it in a Syrian refugee camp, or a run-down council flat on an estate where 60% of the people haven't been able to find regular work for two generations, or to answer it as a Christian in a country where you risk your life just by going to church.

So, the ideal answer would have to address the big questions, like what we're living for, what kind of people we want to become, what kind of contribution we want to make, what kind of society we want to see. And it would have to give us simple criteria for answering all the little questions we face every day – where to live, what to eat, what to drink, what to buy, how to travel, how to use our time well, how to choose a job ...

We need a 'lens' that not only helps bring the big picture into focus but also helps us see all the little things with the right perspective. We need bifocals.

This book is about one man's answer to that question, an answer that is like that wonderful moment at an optician's when, having already popped a variety of lenses into the machine, they slide in the last one, and you can tell a 'u' from a 'v' and an 'e' from a 'c', from a hundred yards.

There's the story, a true story as it happens, of a teacher of the law asking a carpenter – a builder really – this question: 'What is the most important commandment of all?'

Now the carpenter had acquired such a reputation for teaching that, despite having no formal education or qualification, most of the people of his time addressed him as rabbi. His reply is the key to the good life, the key to a better society and the key to the restored heart – the best idea in the world.

Of course, in an age of media hype and advertising huff and puff, it's hard for us to take claims about the best or the greatest too seriously. After all, we've had endless lists ranking the best and the worst of everything – from films to futons, from the rich list to the hitch list, from goal of the season to blouse of the year, from the top 100 best ads to the top 100 places to eat quinoa in Quebec. Still, for many a man and woman in first-century Israel, the question, 'What's the most important commandment of all?' was of great significance. Nor was the man who asked the rabbi Jesus that question the only person recorded posing it (Matthew 22:34–40). Clearly, it was an important question.

And it wasn't necessarily an easy question to answer. After all, back in the first century AD, there were rather a lot of commandments for a devout Jew to choose from. Not just the Big Ten, but some 613 that the rabbis had identified. It's one thing to look for a needle in a haystack; at least the needle is qualitatively different from straw and you can always use a magnet. But choosing one from among 613 divinely ordained commandments might appear to be more akin to trying to pick out the best pearl from a bucket of perfect pearls.

Nevertheless, despite having more commandments to choose from than flavours of Jelly Belly jelly beans, Jesus, the rabbi-carpenter, replies with an answer that is swift, simple and succinct, unembellished by parable or delayed by questions of his own:

"'Love the Lord your God with all your heart and with all your soul and with all your mind and with all your strength.' The second is this: "Love your neighbour as yourself."'

MARK 12:30–31

Jesus' answer doesn't come as a surprise to the teacher of the law. Actually, looking back on it 2,000 years later, it still doesn't seem that surprising: 'love God' – that's the first commandment and the second sentence of the *Shema*, the national prayer that every Jew would have known. And 'love your neighbour', well, that summarizes the essence of six-and-a-half of the other commandments which all relate to how one treats one's neighbour – not making them work on the Sabbath, not stealing from them, not wishing to acquire anything that they have.

What's brilliant here is not that Jesus comes up with something new but that he so succinctly and directly summarizes the heart behind all God's instruction. It's obvious. And yet liberating because it's so clear, so simple. Indeed, the questioner's response to Jesus' answer is immediate, congratulatory, honouring, joyous really: 'Well said, teacher.' And he goes on to highlight why: 'to love your neighbour as yourself is more important than all burnt offerings and sacrifices'. In other words, active love for a neighbour is more important than all the rituals and rites of the Temple in whose very courts they were standing. It's like standing in the foyer of the HQ of the largest soft drinks manufacturer on the planet, Coca-Cola's gargantuan complex in Atlanta, and being asked by their senior vice president in charge of marketing, 'What's the most important beverage in the world?' and replying, 'Water.'

You can't make Coke without water. And you can't love God without that expressing itself in loving your neighbour. Indeed, love for God that doesn't express itself in loving your neighbour is as unpalatable to God as globs of undiluted Coke syrup.

Jesus' questioner agrees wholeheartedly, but perhaps he doesn't see the extraordinary implications of what Jesus is saying. 'Oh, yes,' the man might have thought, 'we know that. You're right. But there's nothing so desperately radical about that. I know God is to be loved with all that I am and all that I have. And I know that I am to love my neighbour. Life can perhaps go on as usual.'

Similarly, today there's hardly a Christian in the Western world who wouldn't agree with Jesus' call to 'love your neighbour'. Actually, there's probably hardly more than one human in a hundred anywhere who wouldn't agree, even though there are many who wouldn't agree with the command to love God. Not many people take serious issue with the call to 'love your neighbour as yourself', even if they might actually go about loving their neighbours in somewhat different ways. However, it is one thing to know something and quite another to work out the implications of an idea so familiar, so taken for granted, that it no longer has much force in reality, no longer really shapes the way we live our lives.

Now, of course there are many fine, enriching books about the great commandments that merit careful reading and reflection. This little offering doesn't attempt to cover all the same ground. Rather it seeks to explore the lenses these commandments give us not just for our personal relationships but for their liberating implications for every aspect of our lives – private, communal, national and international.

In fact, Jesus' response is perhaps even more radically countercultural today than it was 2,000 years ago. To a culture trying to push God to the periphery, Jesus says, 'Put God in the centre.' Because human beings are spiritual beings. To a culture obsessed with rights and the dead-end trinity of me, myself and I, Jesus says, 'Focus on others.' To a culture suffering from epidemic levels of loneliness, depression and alienation, Jesus says, 'Focus on community.' To a culture obsessed with acquiring quality things, Jesus says, 'Focus on building quality relationships.'

Indeed, the simplicity of Jesus' answer should not distract us from its significance. If these are the most important commandments, then they reflect what is most important to God. What, then, is most important to God? *How we love.* How we love him and how we love our neighbour. And love is fundamentally about relationship.

So the thing that is most important to God is:

1a. The quality of our relationship with him.

1b. The quality of our relationships with others.

Christianity is not a 'system' to be followed, a body of rules to obey, hurdles to jump or boxes to tick, but a particular kind of friendship with God and people. Of course, at first glance, this focus on relationship sounds all rather fluffy and vague, but, as we shall see, the call to love is not a call to sit around meditating on eternal truths in a blissful reverie, but rather a summons to become involved in a down-to-earth movement to make the world a better place. Romantic love may begin with a walk in the park, but it ends up with a discussion about who's going to pick up the kids from school this afternoon. True love is not just about drowning in the intoxicating gaze of the beloved, but about making decisions, doing things for our beloved that makes their life better. Indeed, if you love someone, you think about the impact on them of everything you do and say. If you love someone you want the best for them – the best education for them and their kids, the best health care for them and their kids, the best air, the best water, the best nutrition, the best opportunities to grow and flourish. If you love your neighbour, who's 67 and lives in a village that's five miles from anywhere and ten miles from a pharmacy, you don't want the bus service that's her only way out of the village to be reduced to one bus at 3 o'clock on a Wednesday afternoon. If you love your neighbour, who's a co-worker in the same shop, you don't want to see him snipped and sniped at by some bad-tempered, capricious boss. You want to find a way to change the dynamic.

So then, against God's most important criteria, how am I doing?

How is my relationship, my adventure with God?

Even the question brings me up short. How is it, *really*? Deep, dynamic? Or distant? Excited or indifferent?

How is my family doing? Do we relate well? Yes, we love each other, we're family. But are we like the Finns who, when asked whether the Russians are their friends or their brothers, tend to reply: 'Our brothers. Because

ROMANTIC LOVE MAY
BEGIN WITH A WALK
IN THE PARK, BUT
IT ENDS UP WITH A
DISCUSSION ABOUT
WHO'S GOING TO
PICK UP THE KIDS
FROM SCHOOL THIS
AFTERNOON.

you can choose your friends.' Is there anything truly dynamic, purposeful or enriching about the way we relate? Sometimes I wonder whether I am really helping my kids grow as people, or just servicing their food, financial and transport requirements. How easy to let mealtimes become mere pit stops between school and homework. How easy for me to let the sheer number of times I have to drive my teenagers to their interminable swimming sessions in overheated, chlorinated halls turn into a chore rather than a great opportunity to chat, chill, listen to music they like and try to like it too, and sometimes find out what's really going on in their lives.

And what about my relationships at work? After all, apart from some romantic liaison, the very idea of 'love' in the workplace sounds like an alien concept. But if my relationships with the people I spend so much time with are not characterized by any genuine, benevolent interest, what does that say about me? Am I just there to share the carpet, collect my pay cheque and one day maybe attend their funerals, only to realise that I knew nothing much about them except that they liked to leave their tea bag in their cup until the water was the colour of coal, but then still add lots of milk?

And at church, what is the quality of relationships there? Yes, we know we're meant to love one another. But what does that mean exactly? Is there more to it than polite affability? Safe, social but superficial. And if I'm in a group – small group, cell group, house group, connect group, life group, youth group, midweek mums, missional community – whatever we now call it, what do I really know about them?

About their life history? About the fiancé that got away, the mum that left, the dad they wish they had? Do I know the name of their boss, or their tutor at uni, or their best friend in all the world? Often we enter people's lives at a particular point and never find out much about what happened before that, or even what's really important to them now.

I wonder, when you think of the quality of your own relationships and the quality of relationships in your town or your nation, what word or thought pops first into your mind?

Loving?

No road is long with good company.
TURKISH PROVERB

*The groundbreaking 2017 meta studies came to two important
conclusions; greater social connection was associated with a
50% reduced risk of dying early and the effect of loneliness had
an effect on the risk of dying younger equal to that of obesity.*
QUARTZ MEDIA, JANUARY 18TH 2018

Either friendship or death.
THE TALMUD

*There's no better way to dismantle a
personality than to isolate it.*
LADY DIANA, PRINCESS OF WALES

CHAPTER 2

THE DISCONNECTED HEART

or

HOW TO AVOID PAYING FOR EVERYONE'S DINNER

They're making a lot of noise, this group at the back of Vittorio's restaurant, not rowdy, *yet*, just the kind of decibels you'd expect from a gaggle of young twenty-somethings out for dinner – exclamations of mock outrage, guffaws, laughter, sudden booms of high volume as they all try to get their line in at the same time. And then interludes when it goes strangely hush as all attention is turned to one person – interludes that tend to be rather short.

The table is full: plates, tall water glasses, a couple of wine glasses, a jug, a lone Peroni bottle, a bread basket, crumpled cellophane breadstick wrappers, and there, right in the centre, by the giant wooden pepper mill, a pile of mobile phones.

They have a rule, this group of friends: mobiles off, mobiles in the centre of the table, and if you use your mobile, you pay for everyone's meal. And, since this is a group of students who have to think twice about going out to eat to celebrate their friend's birthday, nobody is going to be using their mobile.

They're not anti-phone, not anti-technology; they just know what a bong, a bing, a beep, a drum roll, a throbbing vibration in one's pocket, or three bars of 'Uptown Funk' can do to a conversation: kill the moment, kill the flow, kill the mood, kill the other person's concentration ... and it's not worth it.

At another time, in another place, these phones may well enrich their relationships – enable them to hear Mum's voice, see Grandad's face, be part of a work meeting that's happening in eight countries simultaneously, enjoy a picture of that ridiculously cute chocolate brown Labrador pup, a WhatsApp shot from their brother of Muse on the Pyramid stage at Glasto, a shared Tweet from President Trump claiming to be the most popular man on the planet ... but right now, and in pretty much any live conversation, the phone isn't a facilitator, it's an immobilizer. Worse, it's a grenade.

The reality is that it doesn't really matter if you have the conversational skills of a chat show host, if you want to have a decent conversation, you have to create the right conditions for it. You can't have a proper conversation if you're constantly being interrupted; you can't recite a sonnet in the middle of a dance floor with the volume at max and expect a princess to melt. It takes more than good relational skills to develop and nurture the kind of friendships and communities we yearn for. We also need the ability to manage and change our physical and cultural environment. The context around us either makes it easier to connect – or more difficult. And once you understand the dynamics of your context you can respond. People who lead teams of remote workers are indeed finding innovative ways to build connections between people who are doing good things together but may never shake each other's hands.

Global Cooling

That said, sadly, the soil and climate of Western culture is increasingly, if unintentionally, hostile to the kind of good life many people yearn for. Our habitat is being degraded, and one of the biggest casualties is the quality of our relationships.

Indeed, in the UK, the US and Australia, the quality of our emotional life, our relational life and our community life has rarely been poorer. All the research suggests that we are less happy than we were a generation ago. The recent wave of 'happiness' studies is enough to bring tears to a Tigger. In the UK, for example, we have never been so depressed, or at least we have never taken so many antidepressants – prescriptions doubled from 12 million in 1991 to 24 million in 2001, rose to 40 million in 2012, and then rocketed to 64.7 million in 2016[1]. Our divorce rate is among the highest in Europe, membership of clubs has declined and involvement in community activities has plummeted. Plenty of kids want to become Cubs and Brownies, but the Brown Owls who lead them are becoming rarer than penguins in the Sahara.[2]

As report after report makes clear, British children are unhappier and report lower levels of well-being, satisfaction with family life, school, appearance, self-confidence, and

1 Anna Moore, 'Eternal Sunshine', *The Guardian*, 13 May 2007. https://www.theguardian.com/society/2007/may/13/socialcare.medicineandhealth ; Haroon Siddique, 'Antidepressant use soared during recession in England, study finds', *The Guardian*, 28 May 2014. https://www.theguardian.com/society/2014/may/28/-sp-antidepressant-use-soared-during-recession-uk-study : Denis Campbell, 'NHS prescribed record number of antidepressants last year', *The Guardian*, 29 Jun 2017. https://www.theguardian.com/society/2017/jun/29/nhs-prescribed-record-number-of-antidepressants-last-year .

2 Christopher Hope, 'Girl Guides: Red tape deterring adult volunteers', *The Telegraph*, 17 June 2008. http://www.telegraph.co.uk/news/uknews/law-and-order/2146670/Girl-guides-red-tape-deterring-adult-volunteers.html .

happiness in the last few years than the vast majority of comparable Western European countries.[3]

Even if you dispute the research, even if somehow the UK managed to claw its way up the rankings a bit, you only have to talk to the police or to doctors or to teachers to know that we are rearing an increasingly anxious, disaffected generation. The picture is virtually identical in the US.

Of course, *everyone* knows relationships are important – never more obviously than when they really aren't working; when we're angry, outraged, bitter with the one we love, who we thought loved us … because of something they did or they keep on doing, or something we did and they can't forgive or forget. We know the terrible damage a break up can create. And we see the impact on our friends of living in families that are fractious, touchy. We all know relationships are important. And we know it at work too – the difference it makes just having someone who cares about you as a person at work, the difference a great manager makes. One friend of mine received a letter from an employee's wife thanking him for being the best boss her husband had ever had. Relationships in one place affect relationships elsewhere – the heart bruised at home goes into work bruised; the heart bruised at work goes home bruised. Oh, yes, we all know relationships are important, but if it's so obvious, why is it that so much of the way we live life today has served to undermine the quality of our relationships? Have we just got so used to living with pain, perhaps even increasing pain, that it seems normal, inevitable?

---

3 UNICEF Innocenti Research Centre, 'Child Poverty in Perspective: An Overview of Child Well-Being in Rich Countries', Report Card 7 2007. https://www.unicef-irc.org/publications/pdf/rc7_eng.pdf .

THE HEART
BRUISED AT
HOME GOES
INTO WORK
BRUISED; THE
HEART BRUISED
AT WORK GOES
HOME BRUISED.

In the West we are suffering from an epidemic of loneliness. In January 2018, the British government appointed the first Minister for Loneliness. In fact, 200,000 elderly people report not having spoken to a friend or relative for more than a month.[4] As anthropologist Margaret Mead put it: 'One of the oldest human needs is having someone to wonder where you are when you don't come home at night.'[5] The number of people who don't have such a 'someone' is soaring. Nearly half of people over 65 say that TV or pets are their main form of company.[6] Soberingly, recent research has now proven what many suspected all along – loneliness can be as bad for our physical health as smoking fifteen cigarettes a day.[7]

We may know more people, but we have fewer friends and we spend less time with the people we say are important to us than our counterparts thirty, forty or fifty years ago.

Yet we hardly realize how lonely we are. We stumble upon that aching feeling only when we think about throwing a party and have so few people we really know to invite. Or we move to a new job or lose our job and realize that the relationships we had at work, however agreeable, never created a bond that would survive the loss of daily contact and shared tasks. Indeed, recently I realized that some of the people I consider to be my really good friends are people I actually see only once or twice a year. How on earth did this happen?

---

4 Aamna Mohdin, 'Britain now has a minister for loneliness', *Quartz* https://qz.com/1182715/why-the-uk-appointed-a-minister-for-loneliness-epidemic-leads-to-early-deaths/ .

5 Attributed in *The Quotable Woman* (Running Press, 1991) p.53 .

6 Age UK, 'Evidence Review: Loneliness in Later Life', https://www.ageuk.org.uk/globalassets/age-uk/documents/reports-and-publications/reports-and-briefings/health--wellbeing/rb_june15_lonelines_in_later_life_evidence_review.pdf .

7 Campaign to End Loneliness, 'Threat to Health', https://www.campaigntoendloneliness.org/threat-to-health/ .

We have a myriad of ways to communicate with people (and their avatars) – mobiles, texts, emails, webcams, instant messaging, blogs, Twitter, Facebook, Instagram, Snapchat, WhatsApp, Skype, Zoom – and yet we feel out of touch, disconnected from the kinds of relationships that thrill our souls and give our spirits wings. We are globally wired but relationally disconnected, touched a million times a day but rarely embraced.

Trust and Profit

Not surprisingly, perhaps, we also trust other people much less. And this has had a significant effect on the quality of our working lives. Even before the 2008 credit crunch, there was a crisis of trust in English-speaking Western societies that deeply affected the profitability and effectiveness of almost all our institutions and businesses. One of the keys to sustainable profitability for a business, according to research, is the extent to which people trust their managers. Low trust, low motivation. High trust, high motivation. High motivation, higher performance. Gallup surveys have shown that one of the three most important indicators of job satisfaction is whether someone in the organization actually cares about the employee as a person.[8] Many people don't leave their jobs, they leave their managers.[9] And high turnover costs money in recruitment, in training, in lost productivity. Relationships really, really matter to the bottom line.

---

8 Marcus Buckingham and Curt Coffman, *First, Break All the Rules: What the World's Greatest Managers Do Differently* (New York: Pocket Books, 2005); 'Feedback for Real', *Gallup Management Journal*, 15 March 2001. *http://gmj.gallup.com/content/811/Feedback-Real.aspx* .

9 Brigette Hyacinth 'Employees don't leave Companies, they leave Managers', Linkedin, 27 December 2017. https://www.linkedin.com/pulse/employees-dont-leave-companies-managers-brigette-hyacinth .

This decline in trust has had a similar impact on investment. After all, if you don't trust the numbers on the balance sheet, you won't invest in a company, and if companies are starved of investment, they are unlikely to grow. Sadly, the financial crises of 2008 and 2009 only served to accelerate a trend that was already there. Ten years on, it's hardly imaginable to many people that there was a time when the banker in a sombre dark suit was the epitome of trustworthiness. While, no doubt, 99% of the people who work in banking are people of high integrity, trust in the institutions they work for and the people who lead them has plummeted as big bank after big bank has been hit with multibillion-dollar fines for malpractice. Overall, trust has been melting faster than the polar ice cap.

This applies to social media as well, where fewer than a quarter of Britons trust Facebook or Twitter. Conversely, the rise of fake news has gone some way to restoring trust in mainstream news outlets but levels of actual engagement in the daily news agenda is falling fast – only 6% of the population now describe themselves as 'informed' which is a record low.[10]

Trust in politicians collectively has also declined. Whatever our particular political convictions, the election of property magnate Donald Trump to the White House, the elevation of business entrepreneur Emmanuel Macron to the French Presidency, and the pundit-defying electoral performance of conviction politician Jeremy Corbyn all speak to a decline in trust in party-machine politics and a

---

10 Matthew Moore, 'Trust in social media hits record low amid fears over fake news', *The Times*, 22 January 2018. https://www.thetimes.co.uk/article/trust-in-social-media-hits-record-low-amid-fears-over-fake-news-tczfmpwj5 .

growing thirst for authenticity, plain speaking and personal passion in those we want to lead us. As Will Walden, head of government relations at Edelman UK, said:

> *We forget we are at the tail end of a decade that began with the financial crisis and ended with the division over Brexit. Distrust is now the default position. Politics doesn't matter to people in the way it once did. What matters is a sense of accountability and follow-through, delivering on policy promises that help ordinary people, and communicating honestly and transparently. This is true of both Remainers and Brexiteers.[11]*

In sum, thinking about the impact of decisions on relationships matters not just in our private lives, it matters in the public sphere – to our work and to our nation's politics. Fundamentally, the primary role of politicians should be to help create conditions in which people can flourish as whole human beings in an ordered, benevolent society.

Creating good relationships then is not an end in itself. It is a means to a higher goal. Yes, Jesus comes to give us a way to have peace with God, to enable us to be reconciled to God, his enemies though we once were (Romans 5:10). He came to make 'peace through his blood, shed on the cross' (Colossians 1:20). So, just as *all* things, visible and invisible, were created by and for Christ (Colossians 1:16), so by his blood, by giving his life for ours – yours and mine – he

---

11 Edelman, 'Social Media on Notice as Public Calls Out Insufficient Regulation'. https://www.edelman.co.uk/wp-content/uploads/Website-Edelman-Trust-Barometer-Press-Release-2018.pdf .

initiates the reconciliation and renewal of *all* things – visible and invisible (Colossians 1:20). So, this 'peace', as expressed in the Old Testament in the Hebrew word *shalom*, is much more than the absence of war, or even conflict, much more than an inner, or an ethereal, serenity.

In the New Testament 'peace' is used in a variety of ways. In Philippians 4:6–7 the focus is on freedom from anxiety, on psychological and emotional peace. In Paul's letter to his Christian brothers and sisters in Rome 'peace with God' is a way of summing up personal salvation: 'Therefore, since we have been justified through faith, we have peace with God' (Romans 5:1).

However, in its richest understanding, this peace, this *shalom* is wholeness, is fullness, is an encapsulation of all things being as they should be. *Shalom* is not just peace with God – theological – it is peace that embraces every aspect of time and matter. It is economic, political, ecological, inter-racial, intergender, international, global, cosmic, relational, physical, mental, emotional, spiritual … *shalom*. Now you can't have shalom without good relationships … but you can have good relationships without *shalom*. You can be a relationally rich, close-knit, loving family of four, living in one room in a bed and breakfast in Oldham … but without a job for either parent, without a desk for the eight-year-old to do their homework, without connections to the wider community, without a place to play … that's not *shalom*.

In sum, good relationships are more than an end in themselves. They are both an end in themselves, and a means to an end. And it is Christ's death that brings about cosmic, eternal *shalom*.

So, for us all, citizens and political leaders, there is a bigger goal. Government policy should aim at *shalom*. However, in the US and the UK the overall thrust of government policy has actually created conditions that have made us unhappier than other 'developed' nations. We have pursued a form of capitalism that is much more concerned with economic growth than it is with the social impact. By contrast, continental European capitalism is much more relational. It's a curious thing that the countries in Europe that have the happiest children and the happiest adults are the ones where the taxes are highest and the CEOs are paid much less, relative to their employees, than in the UK and the US.

Who's happiest? The Norwegians, the Danes, the Icelanders, the Swiss and the Finns.[12] And it's certainly not because of the weather. There's something in the culture that means that people don't feel the need to earn 500 times more than a junior employee to want to lead a great company. Or feel the need to leave their country to land that kind of salary. And that applies at every socio-economic level. There's something in the culture that means that people actively want their neighbour to be able to live in reasonable comfort, even if it might mean that they themselves don't have two foreign holidays a year. There's something in the culture that resists the trend to sixty-hour working weeks, that values time with family and friends highly enough to create an overall environment in which it is protected.

---

12 Sustainable Development Solutions Network (SDSN), J. Helliwell, R. Layard, & J. Sachs, 'World Happiness Report 2017', http://worldhappiness.report/ed/2017/ .

One non-relational thing after another

Sadly, in the UK, the last thirty years have seen the introduction of a myriad of social policies and trends that have combined to create a culture that doesn't seem to value those things, that has served to undermine the quality of relationships. We've seen urbanization and suburbanization, school relocations outside neighbourhoods, the closing of local hospitals, a decline of 'live' entertainment venues, a rise in single-parent families, a rise in two-parent-working families, all of which, if nothing else, means that adults spend less time with their children.

It doesn't have to be that way. On Thursday December 17th, 2017, I read an article in the *Daily Mail*[13] celebrating the fact that The Entertainer, the biggest independent retailer of children's toys, would not be opening their stores on Christmas Eve – the day with the highest turnover in the entire year. It would cost them an estimated £2 million in lost profit. That year, Christmas Eve fell on a Sunday. And The Entertainer hasn't opened their shops on a Sunday from the time they only had two stores. They now have over 140 stores. And they don't open their stores on a Sunday for two reasons. The second reason is this: the owners want to spend time with their family and friends when their family and friends are free to spend time with them, and they want the same thing for everyone who works for them. The first reason is this: God told the founder, Gary Grant, not to open on a Sunday. Gary is loving God and loving his neighbour.

---

13 Jonathan Petre & Mark Branagan, 'Hallelujah! Selfless shopkeeper is closing his Entertainer toy stores on Christmas Eve because he does not open on Sundays - even though it will cost him £2MILLION', Mail on Sunday, 17 December 2017. http://www.dailymail.co.uk/news/article-5187233/Shopkeeper-closing-Entertainer-stores-Christmas-Eve.html .

People in the retail industry thought he was stupid. People in the toy industry thought he was nuts. People who work for him are rather grateful.

Of course, lots of people don't seem to have a choice any more about when they work. Decisions are often taken that make things relationally harder. And there's not much many of us can do about it. Rising house prices mean living further from work. And ever-increasing commuting distances mean that we're away from our homes for a greater proportion of the day and have less time not only for friends and family, but also for community activity.

Similarly, our isolation has also been increased by the introduction of a host of new technologies – many wondrous in themselves – but which nevertheless reduce the amount of time we spend building friendships. In the US the average household now has more ways to stream screen entertainment than people.[14] The two PC, four mobile, one PlayStation, two iPad household is alive and well and here to stay,[15] no doubt soon topped with the arrival of four virtual reality headsets. All of this is, of course, incomplete without in-car Wi-Fi film streaming to fend off the psychological trauma of long and winding journeys playing 'I spy' and singing along to songs on the radio or, heaven forfend, actually talking to the ageing 'chauffeur' in the front. Increasingly, individual members of families are locked away in their own worlds – real or

14 Laura Hamilton, 'How many active connected devices does a home in North America average?' CED magazine, 24 August 2016. https://www.cedmagazine.com/data-focus/2016/08/how-many-active-connected-devices-does-home-north-america-average .

15 Press Association, 'Online all the time – average British household owns 7.4 internet devices', The Guardian, 9 April 2015. https://www.theguardian.com/technology/2015/apr/09/online-all-the-time-average-british-household-owns-74-internet-devices .

virtual – and the number of things they do together has plummeted. Of course, there's nothing intrinsically wrong with these technologies but, in most cases, the more there are of 'them', the fewer there are of 'us'. Most people would rather talk to friends than watch TV, but most people spend more time watching TV than talking to friends. We are losing the art of conversation.

Of course, deep relationships have never been that easy to develop, and I'm certainly not suggesting that there was some golden age of relational paradise. Still, the way that Western society currently operates makes rich relationships much harder to develop and maintain, quite independent of any of the personal challenges most of us face in nurturing the relationships we'd like. In the West, we're in a desert. Sure, things grow, but there are a lot of spikes around.

Why this decline?

It's surely not because there are millions of people out there who actually relish poor relationships. Of course, it's complex. And whilst we will look at some of the convictions and decisions that have made things worse, there is still the reality of our human nature. When Adam and Eve rebelled against God in the Garden of Eden they didn't just hide from God, they started to hide from each other – they put on clothes, so they couldn't be fully seen. That's what fear does. Fear makes me worry about me, about my worth, my personality, my attractiveness, my biceps, my trainers … Fear puts me before you, makes you dangerous: you could hurt me, you might find out about me, what I am really like, you might reject me, talk about me to others, put me down in class, in the canteen, in the office, online … oh, God, online … that dumb comment, that terrible picture

FEAR
PUTS ME
BEFORE
YOU.

on and on and on and online, forever. And that's our contemporary challenge: our technology can turn some tiny error, or indeed no error at all, into a public shame-fest. Fear. So our technologies can put us under more pressure. Many companies train their people on the appropriate use of technologies; more and more schools have rules about the use of social media. In sum, we no longer take it for granted that people know how to protect their privacy from prying eyes or themselves from personal attack.

Perhaps part of our historic problem (quite independent of the challenging times we live in) is the reality that we take for granted that we know how to build, maintain and protect good relationships. That we have a full complement of relational skills; that we know how to listen well, that we know how to give and receive feedback (one of the first skills McKinsey[16] teaches their new graduate employees), that we know how to forgive and to ask for forgiveness. Most of us, for example, assume we're good at listening. After all, listening is the first communication skill we learn. We acquire it in the womb, and don't pay much more attention to it afterwards than we did then. Not many of us read books about it, or take courses in it. And yet, not many of us are great at it. Maybe it's the same with relationships. We begin relating in the womb, and unless some crisis hits or we have some professional incentive, we don't spend much time deliberately developing our skills or studying it, never mind learning to consciously apply a relational lens to our decision-making.

---

16 'How to give McKinsey-style feedback: The McKinsey Feedback Model' on 'Working with McKinsey', November 15 2012. http://workingwithmckinsey.blogspot.co.uk/2012/11/giving-mckinsey-style-feedback-model.html .

More broadly, in many businesses and institutions the quality of relationships is essentially ignored. After all, what do relationships have to do with maximizing productivity, profitability and shareholder value? Actually, as it turns out, a great deal. Similarly, in our private lives, though most of us know that relationships are important, we find it hard to live that way. In a culture that vaunts the individual and has done so much to erode community, we have not developed the tools to help us predict the likely impact of our decisions on our relationships.

Logos R Us

Yet our thirst for intimacy continues undiminished and unsatisfied. Cut off from any vibrant connection to the divine, and increasingly impotent to form relationships of intimacy, Western culture has given its thirsty heart to the obsessive acquisition of things and the anxious, approval-seeking display of logos. I display therefore I am. *Logo ergo sum.*

Psychologically, this seems like a regression to an infantile stage. When mothers begin to wean infants from the breast, the infants are often given an object – a blanket, a teddy bear, a wooden spoon – that becomes a comfort to them, a substitute for the close relationship they enjoyed with their mothers. And this object often accompanies them for months, even years. The object becomes a surrogate, a temporary substitute for the relationship they yearn for.

Most children grow out of this. Western culture has not. We try to substitute objects for relationships. There's a good reason why 'Thou shalt not covet' makes it into God's top-ten commands. Coveting breeds discontent: it's an expression of the lie that what *other* people have is essential to my well-being. The command, after all, does not say 'thou shalt not desire a wife', or that the wish to own an ass to help carry produce to market is anathema to the God who created the ass. It says don't *covet* your neighbour's wife, house, ass … Coveting, therefore, introduces an elemental, even if often low-key, resentment towards my neighbour, and an entirely inappropriate diminishment of ourselves. Comparison-shopping may help you get the best deal; comparison-living is the highway to anxiety and self-loathing.

Rebooting the Relational System

Jesus' response to the teacher's question – 'Which is the most important commandment?' – directly addresses these issues: the personal, the cultural and the political. In the following chapters, we will look at some tools to help us apply Jesus' focus on relationships to everyday life, and we'll explore something of what he actually meant by 'love' – a word so devalued in our culture that it is almost bereft of meaningful content.

Jesus' No. 1 principle, however, isn't just a helpful piece of wisdom that might make your life a bit better or your business more profitable. Jesus' response reflects the very essence, not only of his teaching, but of the nature of God. Life, and indeed Christianity, is meant to be lived in meaningful relationships. As such, relationships are not an optional extra to the good life – they are utterly essential.

COMPARISON-
LIVING IS THE
HIGHWAY
TO ANXIETY
AND SELF-
LOATHING.

'Love God, love your neighbour' reflects the heart of the heart of all that really matters.

Importantly, it not only clarifies God's priorities, it provides a tool for us to consider almost anything we do. After all, the command to 'love' is a relational command. As we've seen with the example of turning off mobiles in a restaurant, when we ask how a decision might affect our relationships with people, suddenly it helps us see the benefits and the pitfalls more clearly. As we shall see later, asking the question about how something affects our relationship with God yields similar insights.

Furthermore, the relational lens is not only a means of examining our own behaviour, it is also a diagnostic tool in analyzing everything from karaoke to housing policy.

Should we in Britain, for example, have built those sixties concrete tower blocks that came to dominate our inner-city skyscapes? They weren't bad because they were ugly – they aren't. At least not from a distance. They weren't bad because they were an inefficient use of space or funding. Functionally efficient they were – the modernist's dream realized in concrete. They were bad because they failed to preserve or create vibrant, safe communities. They became relational deserts where delinquent jackals prowled, and neighbours did not know each other – contexts without community spirit – with graffiti on the walls and needles in the vandalized playgrounds. The design didn't serve to nurture relationships but rather to make them more difficult.

Design affects relationships.

Sometimes positively. Sometimes negatively. If you build housing units, as some builders have done, in which there is no space to put a table for a family to eat round, is it any surprise that family relationships suffer? If, in a country where people live in smaller houses, the church sells off its spacious vicarages in order to release money for other projects, have they perhaps not also just squandered one of the most important assets they had – a house big enough to host those parties, large Bible studies, prayer meetings, bring-and-share lunches that serve to build better relationships in community? Selling off the vicarage may be the right decision, but considering the relational dimension highlights what may be lost or gained.

Since almost everything we do, every decision we make, affects relationships in some way, what more specific guidelines can we bring to bear to analyze the current health of our relationships and assess the likely impact of decisions we make?

Shared joy is a double joy:
shared sorrow is half a sorrow.
SWEDISH PROVERB

Eating meals together as a family is a
predictor of educational attainment.
KEEP TIME FOR CHILDREN

The most terrible poverty is loneliness
and the feeling of being unloved.
MOTHER TERESA

CHAPTER 3

GETTING RELATIONAL THINKING TO WORK

or

THE POWER OF CHOCOLATE

Not so long, long ago in a company not particularly far, far away, a young scientist called Anita pondered the utter absence of relationships in her workplace. Every day, the 'team' would come in, suit up in white, and scurry like moles into the single-person labs that the purity of their research required. Occasionally, one of them would scuttle out, take a domestic beaker and mix boiling H_2O with a naturally occurring brown organic compound, rich in caffeine and antioxidant flavonoids. Then they would scamper silently back to their lab to imbibe the solution alone. No one talked to each other, no one shared ideas about the research they were all doing, no one really had much fun. So the young scientist decided to do an experiment and announced that the following Friday she would make hot, fresh-brewed coffee for everyone at 10.30 and she would bring chocolate biscuits.

And so it was that on Friday at 10.30, all the scientists scampered out of their single-unit labs, lured by chocolate, like mice by cheese, into Anita's benevolent conversational trap. Over coffee and biscuits they talked about life, about the news, about their research, about the coming weekend. And week by week, calorie by calorie, the 'team' became more of a team.

When Anita left the company, no one made coffee on Friday mornings and no one brought in chocolate biscuits. Six months later, the situation was so dire that the company hired a management consultancy to do team-building exercises. It cost a fortune. And all they needed was a packet of chocolate biscuits and someone willing to make a pot of coffee.

Anita saw the problem and she identified its cause: people had no reason or permission to meet together. So she created a reason to meet together and gave everyone the kind of direct contact with one another that is essential for good relationships and better work.

Of course, directness of contact is no guarantee of good relationships – you can share a room with a sibling, a co-worker, a spouse and resent every moment of it. Relationships are self-evidently complex and multi-faceted. But there are still things we can put in place to help them flourish.

Relational thinking can sound somewhat theoretical, a little cold even, but it is simply a way of describing what is, or is not, happening. It's obvious that it's hard to develop and maintain a deep relationship without directness of contact. And yet huge numbers of parents spend less than five minutes a day actually talking to their children, and huge numbers of Christians spend less than five minutes a day talking to God.

So, if we want to improve the quality of our relationships, we might ask what things, apart from natural compatibility, tend to contribute to more satisfying relationships.

DIRECT CONTACT
WITH ONE ANOTHER
IS ESSENTIAL
FOR GOOD
RELATIONSHIPS AND
BETTER WORK.

Over the last thirty years, the Jubilee Centre and Relationships Foundation (the Cambridge think tanks founded by Michael Schluter) have identified five factors that tend to predict or lead to what they call 'relational proximity', or closeness.

These factors have also been used to analyze a wide range of types of relationships, not only in families but in companies, in public institutions like prisons and the tax office, with tangible, measurable results. As you read them, you might want to consider how your own relationships – institutional and personal – might be enhanced by these guidelines.

1. Directness of Contact: Maximize It

A kiss on the cheek is better than an 'X' at the bottom of an email, the touch of someone's skin is better than a photo, and a face-to-face conversation is almost always richer than a teleconference. We are made of flesh, not silicon – at least most of most of us are. We are created to relish physical presence, to grow most through direct contact. That's what Anita's chocolate biscuits facilitated – direct contact.

Direct contact almost invariably builds deeper understanding than physical absence. Being physically present is better than sending emails or virtual communication, and usually more effective. This is, of course, common sense. However, such common sense was much challenged in the 1990s and the early years of this century as businesses sought to increase efficiency and reduce travel costs and carbon emissions through increased use of technology. However, true communication is more than the transfer of information. 'Being there' facilitates touch – important even in the simplest of transactions – and increases the accuracy and richness of the communication. Indeed, in any oral communication, words can make up as little as 7 per cent of the message.[17] The rest is voice tone, gesture, body language. There are, after all, lots of ways to say the words, 'Did you buy tickets for the theatre?' Including with an utterly disbelieving, disdainful raising of the right eyebrow.

Directness of contact has proved so vital that a number of businesses have brought back tea ladies, their trolleys and their tinkling bells – not out of nostalgia for ye goode olde days. Quite the opposite. Many businesses found that their employees, like Anita's colleagues, had become bound up in their technologies, sitting in their cubicles, emailing people in the next cubicle and rarely bothering to even try to communicate face-to-face. The result was not only a less satisfying work experience but lower productivity.

However, when the tea lady's bell tinkles, no one has to ask for whom it tinkles ... People have permission to join the queue and chat for a while, sometimes about football, *Modern Family* or the new man in accounts, but often about those little 'by the way' bits of business that are actually more efficiently and easily taken care of directly. In either case, overall levels of communication and camaraderie improve. And so does productivity.

Similarly, in today's office environment, there is almost never a convenient time to spend half an hour eating a sandwich with someone over lunch, even if half an hour is actually only fifteen minutes and it's in a cubicle – dining *al*

---

17 Albert Mehrabian, *Nonverbal Communication*, 3rd ed. (Piscataway, N.J.: Aldine Transaction, 2007).

desko. Besides, as Gordon Gekko famously intoned in the film *Wall Street*, 'Lunch is for wimps.'[18] Nevertheless, over time, spending fifteen minutes munching a sandwich with a colleague once a week can be hugely effective in enhancing efficiency.

Directness of contact is also a useful criterion in the family. How much direct contact do you have? How often do you eat together? And how many of you are there for the whole meal? Talk matters. The bits and bobs, hmmm and grunt talk, the pass-the-salt-how-was-your-day talk, the did-you-remember-whatever-it-was-you-were-meant-to-remember talk, the love-my-non-dairy-blueberry-goo-dessert talk, as well as the I-would-like-to-kill-my-boss/sister/brother, marry-that-guy/change-my-job/I-hate-my-life/where-is-God-in-all-this/let's-move-to-California-dreamin' talk. Talk matters. And it's tough to talk to someone who isn't there or who's watching the TV, as around a third of British children prefer to eat their meals.[19]

So how can you create the kind of dynamics that will build deeper relationships? How can you create opportunities for 'directness of contact'?

In one case, the dishwasher broke. The parents had two teenage children. What should they do?

Have it repaired?

Buy a new one?

They decided to do neither.

Instead, the parents took turns washing the dishes with one of their teenagers.

18 *Wall Street*, directed by Oliver Stone (Los Angeles: 20th Century Fox, 1987).

19 Matthew Smith, 'A third of children eat dinner in front of the TV', YouGov UK. https://yougov.co.uk/news/2017/04/18/third-children-are-eating-their-dinner-front-tv/ .

After all, you are more likely to have an accidental deeply meaningful conversation about life, the universe and the perfect boy/girlfriend with your teenager in the relaxed atmosphere of doing the dishes than in response to the question: 'Why don't we go into the living room and have a nice chat?' Interestingly, when the teenagers left home for university, the parents promptly went out and bought a new dishwasher.

The memorable moments that bring people together – the great laughs, the shared disasters, the wonderful sense of being understood – can as easily occur in a traffic jam, during a frenetic project or doing the shopping as in a chi-chi restaurant or savouring a hazelnut soufflé with the candlelight glinting in your eyes.

Creativity and discernment are required. Buying a 1,000-piece jigsaw puzzle to finish over the Christmas break strikes some people as an advanced form of psychological torture. However, for others, it's a stimulating, cooperative venture that can be nibbled at, left, returned to on your own or in pairs or threes or fours or sevens, and can create precisely the kind of ease that allows conversation to meander from the incidental to the intimate and back again without pressure.

The key issue here is awareness. On the one hand, as we said earlier, we may have a lot of direct contact but may not have found a way to do anything with it – as when I spent those endless hours ferrying my kids to their various activities. When people go to business meetings, they plan what they want to get out of the meeting. What would happen if, as we made our way home, we took a couple of minutes to consider how best to make the most of the coming family meal?

On the other hand, we may simply need to create opportunities for direct contact. That's why some couples arrange date nights and others schedule sex – unspontaneous, even unromantic, as that may initially seem. Still, it has the advantage of valuing that aspect of their lives that is so easily buffeted aside by the gusts and squalls of everyday living. And at least you know when to take a shower. Or get a headache.

Directness of contact also contains a component of intensity. How emotionally and mentally 'there' are we when we're physically there? This idea of 'intensity' explains why some encounters have an impact out of all proportion to the amount of time spent – an extraordinarily intimate conversation on a train with a stranger that you never see again or maybe someone giving you a hug when you really need a hug, for example. Even a stranger. As happened to me once at a speaking engagement when, for reasons that had nothing to do with the response to my talk, I felt raw, wounded, empty of the resources to face what I thought was waiting for me. Then a woman, clearly enthused by what she'd heard, came up to me and asked if she could give me a hug. She really didn't need to ask. The hug lasted less than two seconds, but I've remembered the kindness for a decade.

Directness of contact doesn't guarantee intimacy, but without it you're very unlikely to experience it.

2. Continuity of Contact: Treasure It
I grew up in a little suburb called Northwood on the edge of Greater London. From the age of about ten, my mum

would send me down to the shops with money, a list and a pencil to write down what I'd paid. I'd go and see Mr Allen, the grocer, who was always happy and always knocked a few pennies off the bill, and then on to Mr Worbouys, who looked like a proper butcher, burly and ruddy-jowled and a little bit fearsome. They'd know my name and ask after my mum, and then I'd pop into Carey's to buy eight nails and put it on Mr Greene's account. But now, thirty years later, I have to get in the car, drive four miles, get stuck in the ring road traffic round Watford to have the deep joy of going into some hardware hypermarket called Seek & Queue on the off chance that they might actually have what I want, to be greeted by no one at all, and then scurry round the aisles like a blindfolded toddler in Hampton Court maze, chasing the always receding figure of a salesperson I have never met and who not only doesn't know my name but doesn't know my mother's name either. Only to discover that they don't have what I'm looking for, but that Nails R Us might – which requires another trip round the ring road. And this, I'm told, is progress.

Nevertheless, in the decade or so after leaving home, I'd go back into town and there'd still be people I knew and who would know me and ask after my mum. There was something warming about that continuity of relationship, about there being people you knew and who knew you, even if not necessarily very well, people you felt a definite affection for. But all those shops have closed now, and when I go to the supermarket, the people on the checkout seem to be different every time, and they don't know my name and no one ever takes a few pennies off the bill. Computers don't work that way. Something's been lost.

How arid so many of our sorties into the world now seem. No wonder so many people shop online.

Of course, auld acquaintance is not necessarily best acquaintance, but there's something about old friends – they know just how many times you floated into a room to announce that you'd met the perfect partner, they know how many diets you've been on, they know you were never ever a size twelve, they remember that you were once a great dancer, that you have always had a way with young people, that you lost your first child. You don't have to start all over. Or, in our high mobility, high turnover culture, over and over again. Indeed, as a nation, most of us have fewer friends than our counterparts fifty years ago, and we are much more likely to live more than half an hour's drive away from relatives. And much less likely to work in the same company for ten years, never mind our whole lives.

Similarly, high turnover of staff in public services such as health and social welfare, and GP systems that don't direct you automatically to the doctor you saw previously, can mean having to explain your illness or hardship over and over again, with all the frustration, emotional wear and tear and delay that often results.

Continuity builds trust, not only in the family but in the workplace and in the church. Continuity of presence within a particular community allows a number of relationships to flourish at different levels. Obviously, we can't be best friends with everyone, but after a while just the fact that we have been around people in our work or in our town or club for years develops affection and a sense of belonging and trust.

CONTINUITY
BUILDS TRUST,
NOT ONLY IN
THE FAMILY
BUT IN THE
WORKPLACE
AND IN THE
CHURCH.

Continuity of relationship matters, so when we are thinking about moving jobs or houses or towns or countries, or where we'll retire to, we need to ask ourselves how it will affect our relationships. And whether the relational sacrifice is actually worth it.

3. Commonality of Purpose: Clarify It

It was the end of the season. Not my season, but the end of my son's Saturday morning football coaching sessions. The coaches had decided that there would be a fathers-against-fathers match and that they would join in. The coaches were for the most part under thirty. And the fathers for the most part were over forty. And to the naked eye, and I include myself, we looked somewhat beyond fully fledged matches involving anyone who can run a mile in under a quarter of a day. But, we were told, it would be twenty-five minutes. So we went for it, most of us without boots or anything resembling proper soccer kit.

Of course, this being England, the fathers who had been faithfully watching their progeny from the sidelines had hardly talked to each other for the whole season. Still, as we eyed each other somewhat nervously, there were already the flickerings of an embryonic respect, somewhat suppressed by the more urgent hope that we would a) survive without the need for an ambulance and a defibrillator and b) not play so badly that our sons put themselves up for adoption.

Still, it felt like backs-to-the-wall, not-really-ready-for-the-battle, ill-equipped, not-a-pair-of-Nike-Mercurials-between-us, but, hey, needs must – Dunkirk spirit and all that sort of stuff.

So we huffed and we puffed and the wind blew the ball around. Twenty-five minutes passed. Slowly. But they passed. The whistle blew. Grimaces turned to grins, chests expanded, relief abounded. Then we discovered it was twenty-five minutes *each way*. Huffs turned to wheezes that sounded like chalk across a blackboard, and puffs turned to red-cheeked, doubled-over, hands-on-knees, hurricane-force panting.

But we survived. And as we left the field, something had changed in all our relationships. It wasn't just that that round ball of a man, scarcely five-foot-six and surely overweight, had the agility of a squirrel and the shot-stopping capacity of a truck – it was more elemental than that. We'd all got through this unexpected challenge, and we'd had a good game. So there was a warmth as we left the field, eye contact and genuine smiles as we shook hands. We'd connected. If we'd started the season with the fathers' match, we would have had a lot more fun watching from the sidelines.

Shared activity, shared purpose, shared experience bind people together.

And when we share a purpose, it often diminishes personality tensions or helps to resolve them more quickly when they occur. Wars, for example, tend to focus even the most ethnically diverse nation. Many people who lived through World War II still reminisce about the positive sense of community they experienced. And as President Barack Obama is known to have pointed out, this is one of the reasons that the US politicians who emerged in the post-war years were so much more respectful to one another than the bulk of their successors: they'd fought a war together, they'd put their lives on the line for a cause greater than pretty much any issue they were ever likely to disagree on in Congress.

The impact of commonality of purpose on relationships is also clear in family, community, church and working life. People motivated by a clear common cause tend to be more productive and satisfied. A family that's involved in the 'family' project together and recognizes their shared commitment to helping one another flourish is ever so much stronger than a gaggle of individuals loosely joined by genes, shared facilities and occasional meals.

Interestingly, as it relates to the workplace, an alarming number of workers don't know what's expected of them and how or why what they do fits in with the institution's goals. Employees may have a sense that they are there to make a profit for the shareholders but, beyond that, what is the company's purpose?

Indeed, as Collins and Porras demonstrated in their book *Built to Last*, the most consistently profitable companies are not those that focus on profit but on some higher goal.[20] So people need to know how their work contributes to the realization of that higher mission and to be convinced that the mission is indeed worthwhile. One man is chiselling stone, another man is building a cathedral; one woman is making furniture for science labs, another woman is facilitating the safe pursuit of knowledge for the benefit of humankind; one teacher is teaching kids enough mathematics to get a C, another is helping them grow into

---

20 Jim Collins and Jerry I. Porras, *Built to Last: Successful Habits of Visionary Companies* (New York: HarperCollins, 2002).

ONE MAN IS
CHISELLING
STONE,
ANOTHER MAN
IS BUILDING A
CATHEDRAL.

fully-rounded adults with enough self-respect, enough self-confidence and enough self-knowledge to find a role that contributes positively to humankind.

The same also applies in the church, where an alarming number of people have very little sense of what the church is there to do other than to carry on doing what it is already doing. Indeed, whilst it is certainly true that one of the best things you can do for a lonely person is to give them something to do, particularly if it involves others, people actually need to know why they're doing it. Are they serving coffee because people need a drink after seventy-five minutes in a service? Not a bad reason, by the way. Or are they seeking to facilitate conversations that deepen friendships and open up new ways to encourage one another in the high calling that God has given each one? Is there any sense of how these essential, though mundane, tasks serve the great task of bringing God's love to the world?

Community without purpose is a dead and deadening thing. But shared purpose builds community and releases creativity.

4. Multiplexity: Foster It

Jane was my first boss when I started work in London. She was a tall, elegant, understated English lady, just thirty and not yet married – I've had worse assignments. She had been in advertising since she was eighteen and was just getting into her stride. She ended up as vice chairman and one of the most adored and respected people in the agency. I ended up adoring her too. She seemed utterly at home in the metropolitan world in which she moved – cabs and clients and nice restaurants and a penchant for twinkly things that her salary did not yet give her an opportunity to celebrate. Then she invited me down to her home in the country. It was a little cottage with a smallish garden split between English flowers and a vegetable plot that yielded all kinds of good things and was the beginning of my love for purple sprouting broccoli. And there she was, more at home than in the urban scene, in Wellington boots, not Prada, with thick gardening gloves to protect her parabolic nails, making interesting meals from home-grown produce and taking me on long walks through the Wiltshire countryside. It was in a way a revelation, consistent, of course, with what I knew of her as a person who appreciated the good things in life but making me realize that the range of the good things she appreciated was so much wider than I could have guessed – and so much wider than mine. And so our friendship grew.

People who see one another in more than one kind of context – a multiplexity of contexts – are more likely to develop and maintain deeper relationships. This makes intuitive sense. If I only see a person in one context, in which they are required to play a particular role, wear particular types of clothes, and, in general, confine their conversation to a relatively narrow range of topics, how well will I know them? But if I see them in another context – at a football match, screaming out their lungs in a vein-bursting apoplectic crimson rage at the arrantly unjust and galactic incompetence of an official – I get a different picture. Hence the value of office parties, off-site team-building exercises and excursions to the pub. Or indeed family days. It's quite helpful for people to see where spouses/friends/parents work – even if it's only a desk wedged between banks of filing cabinets behind a pillar in a windowless corridor – as my first office was. (My colleagues called it 'the hutch', not that I'm bitter – the carrots were large.) And it's quite helpful to meet some of the people they work with and for them to meet you: you're real and that secretary he raves about is sixty-two, not twenty-one. Or she's twenty-six, and on a scale of 1 to 10, she's an 11. Now you know what he faces every day.

And of course technology has a role to play in multiplexity. Despite its inevitable limitations the reality is that seeing Grandad on Skype in Melbourne is better than just hearing his voice. Technologies can help maintain established relationships even if there is no substitute for presence.

The value of engaging with people in different contexts also explains the genuine benefit of some corporate entertaining. When I used to work in advertising, I rarely spent my entertainment budget, despite being encouraged to do so. Sadly, there was a little bit of the legalist in me that somehow regarded corporate entertaining as a form of bribery – stick with us and you'll get to go to the US Open. But at its best, corporate entertaining is a legitimate attempt to develop trust by widening the scope of the relationship. Many high-level decisions may well still be made on the golf course or over a pre-theatre dinner. This may not be because senior executives are swept off their feet by the sight of a beetroot and goat's cheese filo parcel but rather because, over a dinner, there aren't usually lots of other people around. In that context, senior executives can say what they think, express a level of doubt or lack of understanding that might be difficult in a meeting with ten subordinates hanging on their every syllable and expecting them to be incisive and decisive. The same applies at any level: the better the relationship, the more likely trust and understanding will grow.

Multiplexity can be applied to families and church contexts too. Has the married couple's relationship been narrowed down to domestic duties and parental responsibilities? How are other important and enjoyable activities preserved? In what kinds of contexts do parents relate to their children? Is it too narrowly confined for parents to get to know their children or for children to get to know their parents? Indeed, there is some evidence that parents with daughters are slightly more likely to divorce than parents with sons. And the reason, given that it tends to be fathers who are required to leave the family home, is that men, though they may love daughters as much as sons, actually feel more bound to sons because they have a wider natural repertoire of leisure activities to share. The old adage was that the family that prays together stays together, but might it also be true that the family that plays together stays together?

Or, looking at a church context, does the church offer her people a range of ways to relate, not simply in what might be called overtly 'ecclesiastical' activities – prayer, Bible study, worship – but in activities that allow people to express other aspects of their humanity – informal suppers, book clubs, sports teams, clean-up-the-neighbourhood days, and even, heaven forbid, quiz nights where you discover that that shy, somewhat retiring individual actually knows more about life, the universe and everything than Wikipedia and has such a comprehensive knowledge of music that they can tell you the name of the bass player on every top-ten album since the invention of the wind-up gramophone. Of course, it may not be immediately obvious how such a discovery might further the cause of the gospel and the transformation of the UK. Still, it's no trivial thing to appreciate other people's enthusiasms and accomplishments. And besides, might they not be the perfect person to introduce to that music-obsessed work colleague that you've been meaning to have round for supper?

5. Parity of Power: Protect It

Her name was Philippa-Jo Dobson, which sounds rather grand, but most people called her Jo. That being her name, I used it too. Still, I preferred to hail her as Jo-Jo, punching the syllables out in exuberant, somewhat infantile delight. Sometimes I'd call her PJD as if our operation were a sleek, platinum paragon of cool corporate efficiency. Jo was our receptionist, events manager and conference manager, and probably a whole host of other things that I, as executive director, even of a small team, was only dimly aware of. That was her job. And she was good at it. My job was rather different. I'm meant to be good at speaking in public, at connecting theology and ordinary life. On my team, I have people with an orbital level of theological acumen, and they help me do things better. We also have experienced speakers and seminar leaders who can not only tell me that something worked well, or didn't work at all, but also spot why.

Anyway, after one evening engagement, I received some feedback from Philippa-Jo through another 'junior' member of staff about what I'd said and how I'd said it. And it was probably the most helpful piece of feedback I'd received in three years. She simply said, 'When Mark speaks, even on a familiar topic, but out of what God is doing in his life at the time, it is so much more powerful.'

Jo is not a trained theologian, though she is very astute theologically. Jo is not an experienced public speaker, though she leads worship in her church. But she, like the rest of the team, is committed to us all doing what we do as well as we can under God. She could have supposed that she shouldn't say anything, and so could the person who passed it on. Still, in healthy organizations, like healthy families, everyone should have parity of power – an equal right to express their opinion, make a contribution, have their voice heard, and feel that they can ask the CEO not to call them PJD or Jo-Jo, if it turns out to be a source of niggling irritation rather than soaring delight.

It is, after all, the powerful who tend to assign people the nicknames that are used in public. And this applies as much to adults as children. Indeed, the principle of parity would mean that 'Big Nose' – a nickname that has been applied to me for reasons which only an elephant or toucan might dispute – gets to choose whether he wants to continue to be called 'Big Nose' and whether that is as appropriate in a board meeting as it is over a meal with old friends.

Of course, people are not equal in their skills or knowledge and so should not have an equal 'say' in how things are run. I don't know a great deal about running conferences. I don't know as much about technology as the director of operations at LICC (The London Institute for Contemporary Christianity). Actually, I don't know as much about technology as the average thirteen-year-old, or the average nine-year-old for that matter. Actually, I don't know much about technology. But I use a lot of it, and whether the technological tools we introduce in my workplace make things easier or more productive is something I have an opinion about. So, as a user, it's important for me to have my say. Similarly, a welder may not know as much as the company finance director about structuring loans, but he or she should certainly have some opportunity to comment on the consequences as they see them for their company. All people are created in the image of God and are worthy of respect and dignity and entitled to a voice.

One person's superior competency in one area should not lead to treating people as inferior beings, nor to the assumption that those less competent in a particular area do not have something to contribute that may turn out to be vital.

Take the 2008 global financial crisis. We had devised a system so complex that it was almost impossible for a non-expert to comment without being dismissed as ignorant. But what we have learned is that 99.98% of the world's financial experts were wrong, that they were not as smart as they, or indeed we, hoped they were. We also learned that the financially unsophisticated people, who had qualms about the ethics of an economy where so much money was being made on money rather than by making products or offering services, were right to be concerned. And we learned that we hadn't found a way to listen to those voices. That's why company suggestion boxes can be a small but significant manifestation of a belief in the parity of power – they concretely express the desire of leaders to listen to the voices of those they lead.

The apostle Paul illustrates the concept of parity by using the metaphor of a body to describe the church (1 Corinthians 12:12–27). Every part is vital, though clearly each part has a different function. The finger may not be as good as a foot at rifling a soccer ball twenty-five yards into the top right-hand corner of the net, but a finger can point out that an opposition player is lurking unmarked on the edge of the box. Similarly, as Jesus pointed out, adults have something to learn from the faith of children, even if he wouldn't have advocated putting a six-year-old in charge of the local synagogue.

This concept of parity has clear implications in a whole host of areas – from family to labour relations. As union leader Tom Jones put it, 'There has never been a strike about pay – only about pay differentials.'[21] People usually don't strike because they want more money, but rather because they feel that they are not getting a fair share of the money available. In other words, people tend to view pay in relational terms. Interestingly, the value of a person's contribution is more important to workers than the ratio between the high and low paid. Workers in companies

---

21 Tom Jones, quoted in Michael Schluter, 'Pay Differentials and Relationships', Jubilee Centre, December 2006. http://www.jubilee-centre.org/pay-differentials-relationships-michael-schluter. Frederick Guy, 'Earnings distribution, corporate governance and CEO pay', International Review of Applied Economics 19, no. 1 (2005): 51–65.

where the pay differentials between junior workers and the CEO are very high tend not to be concerned if they believe that the CEO delivers value.[22] They accept that elite executive talent, like elite sporting talent, can make a huge difference for the whole company. One Ronaldo or Messi or Kane can transform the fortunes of the whole team. One Richard Branson has the capacity to see and follow through on scores of business opportunities that have created thousands of jobs that might otherwise not have existed.

Conversely, it's easy to see why workers and customers become resentful when big salaries are not dependent on spectacular performance, and when huge bonuses can be paid to people who have actually bankrupted the companies they work for. For many people such differentials seem to flout a basic principle of fairness. Similarly, a big company has considerable power to abuse its suppliers by squeezing them on price to the point of unprofitability. The small company clearly doesn't have parity of economic power, but should they not have the right to make a fair profit too?

And this applies in the family. Who has a voice? One of the most countercultural aspects of the Jewish Passover service is the moment when the youngest male child present asks the Four Questions to discover why this night is different from all other nights. The practice dignifies the simplest question. It communicates that we all need to know why we do things, whatever our status. It reminds us

22 Olubunmi Faleye, Ebru Reis and Anand Venkateswaran 'The determinants and effects of CEO-employee pay ratios', *The Journal of Banking & Finance*, August 2013 Volume 37, Issue 8, p3258 – 3272. https://ideas.repec.org/a/eee/jbfina/v37y2013i8p3258-3272.html .
CF Alex Edman, 'Why We Need to Stop Obsessing Over CEO Pay Ratios', *Harvard Business Review*, 23 February, 2017. https://hbr.org/2017/02/why-we-need-to-stop-obsessing-over-ceo-pay-ratios .

that we are all meant to be included, not as mere functions but as people created in the image of God who are part of this unfolding drama in time and eternity.

Later we'll look at how the five criteria might apply to relationship with God, but for the moment, consider your relationships at home, at work, in your local community, club or church. How would you describe them? And what might you do to improve the directness, continuity, multiplexity, priority of purpose, and parity of the ones that are important to you?

In daily life, what we think, what we say, what we feel, what we buy, how we dress affects our relationships – with God and with our neighbour – so considering our behaviour in the light of its consequences on relationships is vital. So yes, we might agree that relationships are really important. But still, we might ask, why does Jesus say that nurturing healthy relationships is the most important thing in life?

You are a person only because of other people.
ZULU PROVERB

CHAPTER 4

TWO'S COMPANY, THREE'S A PARTY

or

A TALE IN TWO PARTS

A Tale in Two Parts – Part 1

Not so long ago, I found myself on the platform at Bond Street tube station. I don't mean to imply by the phrase 'I found myself' that I had no consciousness of how I got there, or that, just a nanosecond before, I had actually been on the Starship Enterprise and had been beamed down by the accommodating Scotty. Or indeed that, like Philip, one of Jesus' disciples, I had moments before been on the road from Jerusalem to Gaza, talking to an Ethiopian eunuch reading Isaiah, and then was suddenly taken up by the Spirit of the Lord and deposited in Azotus, probably around forty miles away. No, the first thing I mean to say by the phrase 'I found myself' is that I was there, as indeed I am wont to be four or five days a week. The second thing I mean to say about the phrase 'I found myself' needs to wait for its moment.

Anyway, there I am standing on the platform with a colleague and listening to the London Transport employee in her blue and orange uniform telling us about the next train. And I'm thinking, 'She's got a good voice and she's using it well.' The announcement is clear, beautifully enunciated without officiousness, pretension or embarrassment. I'm impressed. As the train starts to trundle in, I walk up to her and say, 'You've got a great voice.' In case you're worried for me, I have, I think, reached an age where such actions are unlikely to be viewed as the tactics of a predator.

Anyway, the smile that beams across her face is marginally wider than the train that I scuttle onto.

All of which may seem to have very little to do with the question: Why does Jesus put such emphasis on the quality of our relationships? And the simple answer is that he just can't help it. Any more than Tigger can help being bouncy, Eeyore morose, or Roo mischievous.

I grew up in a Celtic-Pict, Scottish, Russo-Polish, Jewish kind of family. And a very kissy, huggy, touchy kind of family it was. Essentially, my mother had two rules:

1. If it moves, kiss it.

2. If it's still moving, feed it.

She really couldn't help it. Never mind that we were living in the more restrained, cooler environs of middle-class, suburban, southern England, never mind that most of my teenage friends didn't come from a Jewish background, never mind a Celtic-Pict, Scottish, Russo-Polish background … there was no escape. She couldn't help it.

Likewise, the key to really successful recruitment is not to look for people who can do what you want done, but rather to find people who can't help doing what you want done. Ronaldo would have played football even if he'd been born in the 1930s, was being paid fifty euros a week and couldn't afford a dab of Brylcreem, never mind a sleek Italian suit. Similarly, if Kiri Te Kanawa had been marooned on a desert island, she would probably have trilled to the toucans.

Similarly, Jesus can't stop loving and can't stop being concerned about the quality of our loving. For three main reasons:

1. God Is Love

And Jesus is God. And his nature is to love. He just can't help it. That's also why the greatest commandment is 'Love God, love your neighbour', because it's the command that most closely reflects God's nature and most accurately clarifies his priorities.

2. God Loves People

And wants the best for them.

And the best and the most satisfying and significant thing a person can do with their life is to love – to know and enjoy the King of the universe intimately and to give their life to loving him and the people he gives them to love.

Interestingly, research has shown that good relationships are actually good for your health. People of faith, that is people with a relationship with God, live longer, recover from illness more quickly and report better sex lives. Similarly, married people live longer and are happier than the single, the divorced or the widowed and are much less likely to suffer from depression. This, of course, may not be primarily to do with being married but with being involved in nurturing, committed relationships. And that, of course, is just as possible for single people, as the longevity of nuns and monks who live in community suggests. Though, of course, I'm not suggesting that the only paths to long life and happiness are to be found through marriage or monasticism – apparently blueberries and fish oil also help. No, simply put, good relationships are good for you.

3. God Is a Relational Being in Himself

He is three – Father, Son and Holy Spirit – in one.

Precisely how three persons can be one is, of course, a mystery, but it is the picture the Bible paints. God is not some remote Star-Wars-like force in an infinite, impersonal universe, but personal and relational in himself. Indeed, God the Father does nothing on his own but always in relationship with the Son and the Spirit. Yes, the Father creates the universe, but he does so with and by the Son, through the agency of the Spirit.

> *In the beginning was the Word, and the Word was with God, and the Word was God. He was with God in the beginning. Through him all things were made; without him nothing was made that has been made.*
>
> JOHN 1:1–3

Jesus, the Word, is clearly seen as co-Creator, whilst in Genesis we read that the 'Spirit of God was hovering over the waters' (Genesis 1:2).

In his earthly life, Jesus maintains this three-way relationship. At his baptism, God the Father literally speaks

GOD THE
FATHER DOES
NOTHING ON
HIS OWN BUT
ALWAYS IN
RELATIONSHIP
WITH THE
SON AND THE
SPIRIT.

out his approval, and God the Holy Spirit comes on him (Matthew 3:16–17). This Trinitarian initiation is followed by a life that Jesus leads in a dynamic relationship with God the Father. He says, for example, that he only does what he sees his Father doing and only speaks the words he has been given by the Father (John 5:19; 12:50).

Furthermore, it's not just that God is a relational being, it is that he wants to involve human beings in the relationships of the divine community. God may not 'need' our company, but he certainly desires it. So in John 17, Jesus prays for his disciples, present and future:

> *'that all of them may be one, Father, just as you are*
> *in me and I am in you. May they also be in us so that*
> *the world may believe that you have sent me.'*
> JOHN 17:21

The Trinity is not an exclusion zone. Access is not only possible, it is fervently desired. In sum, the Christian understanding is that God is in himself/themselves relational.

This is one of the great distinctives of Christianity. Christianity is essentially a relationship with a person. Not a system, not a set of rules to be followed, but a person to know. This is the heart of the matter. God wants to know us and be known by us.

Could there be a greater affirmation of human worth than the startling truth that the King of the universe, the Creator-Redeemer of all, actually wants a relationship with us? You are not just a cluster of amino acids among seven billion clusters of amino acids on this golf ball of a planet, spinning in an almost infinite universe; you are loved by the triune God who wants a relationship with you in time and eternity.

And he's made that possible through Jesus.

Relationship is so important to God because he is intrinsically relational. And he wants us not only to relate to him but has designed us for relationship with other human beings. Indeed, the first negative note that sounds in the Bible relates to the absence of human relationship. In the biblical account of creation, God pronounces everything 'good' until he says: 'It is not good for the man to be alone. I will make a helper suitable for him' (Genesis 2:18). Of course, at one level Adam is not alone. God is there. And God is not just there in an ethereal sense, he is there in a physical way that Adam can recognize. In Genesis 2 God brings the animals and the birds to Adam to see what he would call them, and in chapter 3 God is described as 'walking in the garden in the cool of the day' (v. 8).

However, despite God's actual presence, it is 'not good for the man to be alone'. To flourish, human beings require not only an environment that provides oxygen, food, drink, opportunity for purposeful activity, for responsibility, for creativity and for relationship with God – all of which God has already lavishly provided – people need relationship with other human beings.

God may be 'enough', but human beings are not designed for that to be the case in their everyday living on earth. Human beings are designed to need others, designed for relationship with others, designed to love and be loved, designed to be interdependent, not independent.

This understanding of who we are as human beings goes against the whole force of Western culture since Descartes said: 'I think, therefore I am.'[23] This statement not only summarized his view that the primary characteristic that distinguished humans from animals was our mental capacity to reason, it also ushered in the age of the individual, the illusion that people can achieve fulfillment on their own and that independence is a high and noble goal.

The Bible stands four-square against this. We love, therefore we are. *Amamus ergo sumus.*

We need others if we are to be fully ourselves. Indeed, when God says that he will make a 'helper suitable' for Adam, he does not mean someone to carry Adam's bags or tidy his desk, he means a person without whom Adam simply, absolutely cannot do the job that he's been given to do. And it's a big job: nothing less than the stewardship of the planet – the release of its potential and the care of its resources. Elsewhere in the Bible the word for 'helper' is applied primarily to God and almost exclusively in situations where decisive intervention is required (Exodus 18:4; Deuteronomy 33:29; Psalm 10:14; Hosea 13:9). This is about a helper who rescues you from disaster, not an assistant who puts the sugar in your coffee.

So, our goal as humans is not a glorious independence but a joyous interdependence, the high adventure of creating a better world through right relationships. We simply cannot achieve what we are designed for without other people.

The isolated human is an aberration.

---

23 René Descartes, *Principles of Philosophy* (1644), part 1, article 7.

WE LOVE,
THEREFORE
WE ARE.
AMAMUS
ERGO
SUMUS.

This is not simply that we cannot fulfill the tasks given to us without others – hunt mammoths, build schools, play tennis – it is that we cannot become who God intends us to be without relating to other human beings purposefully and positively. We cannot love. The person who does not love is less than a person is meant to be. That's why Jesus commands us to love. Selfless love is the only path to fulfillment. Isolation is not good. Community is good. Indeed, when the apostle Paul describes the transformational impact that the Spirit of God is intended to have on people's characters and actions, he begins his list with 'love' (Galatians 5:22–23).

A Tale in Two Parts – Part 2

We are most like God and our true selves when we love.

And that's perhaps why I felt such joy on the platform at the Bond Street tube station. The reality was I felt absolutely great. Much better, as it happens, than the time I gave a train driver I'd just met a note of consolation and a wooden cross after he'd told me, as we walked down the platform towards the front carriage, about his disappointment at not being promoted. No, I felt absolutely great – something akin to pure joy.

I had in a modest way, for a moment at least, done something unselfish, injected a smidgen of appreciative relationship into a situation normally bereft of it. I had acted in the way I should act: honestly, purely and just a little bit courageously. And there was nothing in it for me – except the joy of giving joy. Of course, it was a tiny thing, and yes, loving strangers is often easier than loving a difficult colleague, or a difficult child. I know that taking ten seconds to tell someone they're doing a good job is a lot, lot easier than giving up an evening to serve a meal to the homeless, or once again, and for the umpteenth, countless time, sitting there and listening to a friend pouring out their hurt and grief and anger about the way they are being mistreated, and they *are* being mistreated … Yes, I know that giving someone a compliment is a lot easier than that, but still, finding myself on the platform at Bond Street, I also found myself, for a moment, the more Christlike self I'd like to be more often, when I'm in more challenging situations.

And I experienced something akin to pure joy.

And judging by the smile on her face, so did the tube worker.

But how do we know that joy more often? In more situations? How do we grow in our capacity to let love do its calming work in fractious contexts, let love do its alkaline work in acidic relationships, let love do its regenerative work in desert places?

Can zealous attention to directness of contact, continuity over time, priority of purpose, multiplexity and parity really turn winter into spring?

Interestingly, the carpenter rabbi didn't think so. He always put first things first, even if the gap between first things and second things isn't a gap but an overlap.

For one human being to love another: that is perhaps the most difficult of our tasks; the ultimate, the last test and proof; the work for which all other work is but preparation.
RAINER MARIA RILKE

But as I rav'd and grew more fierce and wilde
At every worde,
Methought I heard one calling, Child!
And I replied, My Lord.
GEORGE HERBERT, 'THE COLLAR'

CHAPTER 5

THE LONG GOOD LOVE STORY

or

MAKING THE DESERT BLOOM

Afterwards it all looked rather different.

I'm twenty-three at the time, sitting in my room in one of the best universities in the world, nursing my bad back and contemplating my impending entrance into the wondrous world of work. And Steve Wexler, a fellow student, asks me if I'd like to pray a prayer that places my life in Jesus' hands.

At the time, it seemed to be about Steve and me and God. But over the years, it becomes clearer. There was Big John and Owen and Graham and Hazel, and a brace of Christophers who all talked to me about Jesus for years, even though I was usually just looking for loopholes in their logic. There was the university missioner I 'beat' in an argument, only years later to realize I'd lost; there were those Christian neighbours to the right of us and to the left of us; there was the Principal of the local Bible college who was one of my father's patients; there was that chaplain at school who told me and another seventeen-year-old boy what he really thought about sex before marriage and, risk of all risks, informed us that he was a virgin and that he expected that his wedding night would probably be the most embarrassing night of his life. There was the drama teacher who cast me as Jesus and the following year as God – it was all downhill after that. There was the senior chaplain who let me lead a chapel service even though I was Jewish; there was the R.E. teacher at primary school who encouraged us to learn all those Bible verses by heart ... Only God knows how many more people, how many beautifully crafted coincidences, how many gentle proddings of his Spirit beckoned me on ...

At twenty-three, perhaps I'd have said that God had been pursuing me for four years. Fourteen years later, perhaps I'd have said that he'd been after me all my life. Now I'd say that the tokens of his love are more numerous than I could list, even if I were aware of half of them ... it's a long love story.

And that's one way of telling the story – the story of a loving God gently but insistently pursuing me, loving me wholly before I had any love for him, any conscious affection really. And of a twenty-something responding to a verbal invitation, my verbal assent expressing mental assent. But it was more than that. Yes, I'd heard the truths about the Gospel, had them explained well and often, but I am not sure how many of them I really understood at that moment ... because at that moment, there was someone else in the room with Steve and me. I know it. It was as if God was drawing me into an embrace, and I was simply surrendering to him, more like a kiss, given and unselfconsciously returned, letting myself lie in his arms, like John the Apostle resting on Jesus' chest. Safe. Loved. God present. God close.

That's how it began for me. He comes to us all differently.

But however he comes, when he commands us to love him and our neighbours, his first step in helping us to do it is by loving us. As John the Apostle himself wrote: 'We love because he first loved us' (1 John 4:19).

And now, having placed that life in his hands, what did he ask me to do with that life? Love him. And love my neighbour. Except to begin with I'm not sure that was at all clear to me. Slowly, some things became clearer – maybe the way I was relating to women my own age wasn't in their best interests – never mind mine – wasn't careful, thoughtful … loving. Of course, he had bigger ambitions for me, as he does for us all, but you have to start somewhere.

The reality is that a life of loving God and loving others, putting God first and actively wanting the best for others, is ever a challenge. It's almost certainly more satisfying than the alternatives, but it's still a really difficult project – loving people in the good times and the bad times, for richer and for poorer, in sickness and in health, loving people when love isn't returned, loving people when you really don't like them, loving people in the way that they are open to being loved even if that is so much less than you'd like to give. But God gives us the resources – the direction, training, ongoing encouragement, empowerment – we need.

And one of the ways he does that is through the Bible, illuminated by his Spirit.

Essentially, the Bible is the story of how the right relationships God yearns for are created, how they are broken, and how he then takes the initiative to help people live with the consequences of their actions and rebuild their relationship with him and with others.

The Blame Game

So, after Adam and Eve turn away from God, the consequences hit their relationships first. They go into hiding. They hide from God when he next comes walking in the garden, and they hide their nakedness from one another since they are no longer comfortable being naked in front of each other. But God comes looking for them and asks Adam, 'Why?' Adam's response is, he no doubt believed, cunning: 'The woman you put here with me – she gave me some fruit from the tree, and I ate it' (Genesis 3:12). It's the first recorded instance of the blame culture. And it's a doozer: Adam not only blames Eve but blames God for bringing her his way.

Humans have been blaming other people, and God, ever since. Indeed, the further a society moves away from God, the more likely it is to become finger-waggingly legalistic and self-righteously litigious. Look at Britain today.

Whilst Adam and Eve's betrayal shatters the perfection of their relationships with God and with each other, God's yearning for restored relationship with human beings is the heartbeat behind all that follows. His determined love flows outwards to people, and through people to other people, and through people into organizations and structures and systems.

With Abraham, God initiates a relationship of promise, making a covenant, a contract with him, as a king might with a vassal, or an employer with an employee (Genesis

17). God promises Abraham and his descendants good things – a land, nationhood, blessing and the high honour of becoming a source of blessing to all people on earth. Abraham is not just a receiver of God's love but a channel for it, a pipeline to all humanity and all creation. In return, Abraham doesn't have to do anything. He doesn't have to pay tribute, or taxes, or meet quarterly performance targets; he just has to trust God and behave accordingly. God's loving blessings are entirely free.

Certainly, later, when God directs Moses to lead the people out of Egypt (Exodus 3:10), away from grinding slavery, mass infanticide and poverty, he sets out a whole range of commands. These commands, however, are not like the labours of Hercules: impossible tasks designed to thwart their happiness and bring about their death. God doesn't rescue his people out of Egypt to torture them, like some cat that has plucked a mouse from a running stream in order to torment and kill it. On the contrary, he's promised them a land flowing with milk and honey – life in abundance.

God's commands are given for people's good. I command my children to pick up the frying pan by the handle – rather than by the side – not because I want to prevent them from discovering the wondrous joys of holding it by the side, but because I don't want them to burn their fingers. So it is with God's commands: they are for our benefit. And they are all relational, designed to help people create a society that will foster human flourishing, that will allow his love to flow outwards.

Importantly, Jesus clarifies not only that 'love God, love

your neighbour' are the two most important commandments, but that all the teaching in the Old Testament Bible
stems from those two commandments. This then is the lens
through which to look at all the other commandments.

So if we take one of the Ten Commandments, such as
'You shall not steal' (Exodus 20:15), and look at it through
the lens of the Great Commandment, we can see that God's
primary concern is not about property but about how theft
reflects a deep disrespect for another person. Theft denies
relationship; theft breaks relationships. The law, then, is
not primarily concerned with the preservation of property
but with the development and preservation of good
relationships between people. Similarly, take one of the
other 613 commands that the rabbis had identified: 'Do not
hold back the wages of a hired worker overnight' (Leviticus
19:13). A hired labourer would not have had any savings, so
he needs his wages straight away so he can feed himself and
his dependants. It's not loving to let a man and his family
go hungry because you can't be bothered to pay him for
work already done. Still, how many bosses actually fail to
pay their employees on time? And how many companies
deliberately pay their suppliers so late that the suppliers go
out of business?

Similarly, the command not to reap to the very edges of
a field or gather the gleanings of your harvest comes out
of love. It expresses God's concern that the poor should be
able to find food, that we recognize our duty of care to those
who don't have enough. It also reflects God's concern that
the rich should not be so concerned to nail down every last
penny of income that they forget either the source of their

income or their duty to be generous to their fellow human beings. Is it 'loving' to pay the people who get up at four in the morning to clean our offices so little that they live below the poverty line, even if they work forty hours a week?

So God says, 'You shall not murder' (Exodus 20:13) because people are valuable to God, and he knows we won't enjoy living in the fear, anxiety and chaos that mar a murderous culture – even if *you* survive. He says, 'You shall not give false testimony' (v. 16) because a culture where lies are told and justice breaks down oppresses people. He says, 'You shall not commit adultery' (v. 14) because adultery shatters relationships. The Ten Commandments are not the ten life-deniers but the ten life-enhancers.

Obeying God's commands is, like honesty, the best policy. Even if in the short term it may not always seem so. Sometimes we obey through clenched teeth, every subatomic particle in our being screaming to go in a different direction: the man who is convinced his wife doesn't love him, hasn't for years, whilst ten yards away is a woman who does, so obviously does, so obviously gets him … oh, what a relief that would be. But will it bring him, or her, good? Will it bring others good? Will it make our community better, or will it be just one more drop of poison in the well that will bring sickness and pain to us all?

Ultimately, obedience to God should not be the grudging, fearful subservience of an oppressed slave, but the willing, willed, trusting response of a son or daughter to a wise and benevolent father.

The Road to Liberation

Jesus puts it this way:

> *'If you love me, keep my commands. [...] Whoever*
> *has my commands and keeps them is the one who*
> *loves me.'*
> JOHN 14:15, 21

The commands of God are good news for people, a 'delight', as Psalm 119:35 puts it. They help to foster intimate relationship with him. And they direct us to the kind of behaviour that will serve to create, nurture and protect healthy, productive, caring, joyous communities, to generate the social capital that is in increasingly short supply. Interestingly, the Bible calls this kind of behaviour 'holiness' (see Leviticus 19). Holiness is often perceived to be an entirely ethereal, otherworldly quality – a smiling, beatific, quasi-elfin aura, a nonchalance in the face of pressure or catastrophe. However, whilst holiness may spring from character, it expresses itself in how we live our daily lives, as indeed the Holiness Code in the book of Leviticus makes clear (chapters 17–26). Ultimately, holiness is love flowing out in thought, word and deed. In corporate social responsibility. In a fair return for tea growers in Assam and seamstresses in Thailand. In befriending the person that no one else talks to in the office. In getting that job or that homework or that manuscript completed on time so that others are not inconvenienced.

Holiness is an expression of love.

Just as the waters of the River Nile break its banks every spring, and flow into the bordering fields, so God's love

HOLINESS
IS AN
EXPRESSION
OF LOVE.

is always seeking to flow out into the world. People may build barriers to it, or channels for it, but either way his love still seeks to reach the withered soul and the parched heart and the arid nation. Indeed, God's concern for the other is intended to flow out beyond the needs of any immediate community, out to the alien, the foreigner, the people who are different to us – in outlook or accent or in the way they dress.

That's why Jesus' injunction to love God and love our neighbour is not only the best idea in the world but the best idea *for* the world. Only the kind of love that flows across borders has the capacity to overcome the rivalries of our riven world.

We, like Abraham, are created to be channels of God's love to others. Treating people well is important to God not just because he is seeking to preserve the harmony and good relationship of existing communities but because all human beings are created in the image of God. All are therefore infinitely valuable to him and worthy of love and care. Indeed, in Jesus' parable of the good Samaritan (Luke 10:25–37), it is not the Jewish priest or the Jewish expert in the law who show compassion for the traveller mugged on the road to Jericho, it is the Samaritan, a man from a community that the Jews of the time despised. Who qualifies as my 'neighbour' is not determined by *their* tribal affiliation, socio-economic status, race, gender, colour or creed, but by what *my* heart is like.

The key question, then, is not who qualifies to be my neighbour, but whether I am 'neighbourly', whether I have a heart of compassion for those in need – whether that's the homeless person outside the supermarket, the secretary with a headache or a Masalit man in Darfur. Jesus doesn't ask us to consider whether a person in need qualifies for our concern, but rather to consider the state of our hearts. He doesn't ask us to calculate what percentage of our income we give away, but to consider what our neighbour's needs are.

Of course, it's possible to devote oneself to a life of praising God but ignoring one's neighbours. It's possible to turn up to church on a Sunday, sing your heart out, and run a profitable business all week that exploits your workers and ravages the planet. It is theoretically and practically possible to pray fervently to the God who said, 'Love your [wife] ... as Christ loved the church' (Ephesians 5:25), and beat your wife. But that is certainly not God's desire. Biblically, you simply cannot love God with all your heart without at least seeking to love your neighbour. Because *he* does.

Love him, love his kids.

Sometimes a misdirected desire to please God can sidetrack us from his priorities. So, for example, Jesus sharply criticizes a group of zealous Pharisees for tithing mint and rue but not looking after the poor (Luke 11:41–42). The Pharisees were so concerned, and probably sincerely so, to 'love' God, to obey God's laws, that they entirely lost sight of his priorities – the poor are more important to God than a tiny pile of herbs.

People before parsley.

Of course, ensuring we have perfectly harmonious relationships with other people is not a prerequisite for a flourishing relationship with God. After all, we can't force people to forgive us. We can only make a determined attempt to bring about the kind of relational reconciliation that God desires, even if sometimes people won't or just can't forgive us. Nevertheless, when they do, it makes you feel like dancing.

Forgiven and Forgiving

Inevitably, other people hurt us – sometimes in terrible, terrible ways. But if we don't deal with the reality of the hurt we feel – the anger, the desire for revenge, the sense of injustice – if we suppress all those feelings and don't find a way to forgive, then the wound festers and its sulphuric pus bursts out in spiteful words, in petty machinations, perhaps in violence. As writer Neil Anderson pointed out, when we are wronged, one thing is clear: we will live with the consequences of what was done or said, whether we like it or not. So the choice we have is whether to live in 'the bondage of bitterness' or 'the freedom of forgiveness'.[24]

In reality, forgiving others is so vital to our own flourishing and to our relationship with God that in the prayer Jesus taught his disciples it is the only command – implicit though it is: 'Forgive us our sins, as we forgive those who sin against us' (Luke 11:4 NLT). If we want to receive forgiveness, we have to be those who are prepared to give it. In other words, if we want to experience God's forgiveness for not trusting him, for failing to live in his ways, for failing to treat people created in his image in loving ways, for taking him for granted, for harbouring resentment against

---

24 Neil T. Anderson, *The Bondage Breaker* (Eugene, Ore.: Harvest House, 1990), 100.

FORGIVING
OTHERS IS
VITAL TO
OUR OWN
FLOURISHING.

others, for believing ourselves to be superior, for thinking about other people in ways that offend the God of love ... if we want to be forgiven our sins, forgive others theirs. And when we do, there are two things we will discover. Firstly, the joy of being forgiven. Secondly, the cost of forgiving. At some level, there is a price to pay – relinquishing a right, resisting the impulse to revenge, refraining from indulging the twisted pleasure of feeling superior, renouncing the joy of setting oneself up in judgement over someone else ...

Forgiveness is the lifeblood of all relationships. Precisely because we all do things that cause damage – deliberately, carelessly, sometimes inadvertently – but damage nevertheless. Seeking forgiveness and extending forgiveness is the only way to continue in our relationships healthily. And that's why we are to be quick to take the initiative to put our relationships in order, whether we've been mistreated or we are the person who's done the mistreating. In Matthew 5:23–24 Jesus puts it this way:

> *'Therefore, if you are offering your gift at the altar and there remember that your brother or sister has something against you, leave your gift there in front of the altar. First go and be reconciled to them; then come and offer your gift.'*

Make it right with people.

Forgiveness does not mean sweeping the issue under the carpet but rather dealing with the mess together. When we don't forgive, we build a wall against love, and it is we who are trapped behind it.

And isn't it such a liberation, such a relief when there are no landmines buried in the space between you and another person? Between you and God? Forgiveness is both an act of love and the vital prerequisite for creating the conditions in which authentic neighbour love can flourish.

Neighbourhood Watch in the Global Village

Jesus' inclusive understanding of 'neighbour love'– defined by *our willingness to be a neighbour*, rather than in our 'neighbour's' nationality, religious affiliation, status or rights – also has profound implications for the way nations interact in a global economy.

In a world in which we not only produce more than enough food to feed every human on the planet but also have the transport capacity to deliver it, it is not loving that one in nine still go to bed on an empty stomach each night.[25] It is not loving to pay a Nicaraguan or Kenyan or Colombian coffee grower so little for their beans that they cannot afford to feed their children, or even roast, grind and drink the very coffee they pick. It is not loving to pay so little to the Malay who makes our clothes – in conditions we wouldn't wish on a rat – that they can hardly afford to clothe their own children.

God is the Creator and God of the whole world, so our concern for right relationships must be global in scope. Individually, we may not, in the short term at least, be able to affect global trade policies, but we can write to our politicians and lobby our supermarkets and buy fair trade

---

25 World Food Programme, 'Zero Hunger'. http://www1.wfp.org/zero-hunger .

bananas – even if that means that we may have to make do with four instead of five.

So holiness becomes real when holiness is expressed both through devotion to God and through loving action towards our fellow human beings.

In the Sermon on the Mount (Matthew 5–7), Jesus clarifies the startling scope of the command to love, calling on those who follow him to love their enemies and to bless those who persecute them. Initially, this seems absurd. How are we to love our enemies? But this is what God does. God's love flows out to all people. He sent his Son for all people, even the enemies who defy him, as we all have done. And so we are to imitate God in loving our enemy, even if their behaviour cannot be condoned or go unpunished.

Furthermore, this is the only way to break the spiral of vengeful violence that ravages so many nations and communities. Nelson Mandela, for example, brought peace to South Africa after the long years of apartheid by choosing to love and forgive the people who had imprisoned and persecuted him and his people. If he had sought revenge, it would have triggered a bloodbath.

Forgiveness is an offer of love to another, an invitation to renewed relationship, a setting aside of the past for the sake of a better shared future. Can we really imagine a good future for our planet or indeed for our own nations without it?

Good Relationships and Good Order

The Bible reveals the long good history of God's determined love, a love with the goal not just of individual intimacy but of global good order and generosity.

Jesus' commands make 'good relationships' the goal of any social system, the goal of the whole world order, where 'good' is defined by the kind of love for God and others he demonstrates. Good, then, not in the sense of affability, but in the sense that the system of relationships is 'good news' for people, regardless of national identity or economic or social status. Government policy should seek to create conditions in which good relationships can flourish, in which populations are drawn together in common goals that benefit all, not just the powerful.

The Christian cannot sit in splendid isolation and simply look after themselves and their immediate family. As Merry said to the Ents, the great trees in *The Lord of the Rings*, when they had decided not to join the war against the Dark Lord: 'But you are part of this world.'[26] The Christian is called to love, to seek the welfare of the company they work for, the town they live in, the society they are a part of and the planet they share. Indeed, this is precisely what God tells the Israelites, who had been forcibly deported to pagan Babylon:

> *Seek the peace and prosperity of the city to which I have carried you into exile.*
> JEREMIAH 29:7

The pursuit of holiness is then the pursuit of intentionally selfless loving relationships and of intimacy with God. And the commandments that God gives are not hurdles that

---

26 *The Lord of the Rings: The Two Towers*, directed by Peter Jackson (Los Angeles: New Line Cinema, 2002).

people need to jump in order to be in relationship with him, but rather loving beacons that show how that relationship is to be lived out day by day in the cultural context of their own time. They show people how to love God. If you want to love me, God says, love your neighbour, your co-worker, your boss, your enemy.

If you want to love me, love my kids. All of them.

And here are some ways to do it.

IF YOU
WANT TO
LOVE ME,
LOVE MY
KIDS. ALL
OF THEM.

All real life is meeting.
J. H. OLDHAM

Q: *'What is the No. 1 casualty of a busy life?'*
A: *'Intimacy with God.'*
KEN COSTA

Love bade me welcome.
GEORGE HERBERT, 'LOVE (III)'

CHAPTER 6

INTIMACY AND THE DIVINE

or

TALES OF FISH AND LIVER

If we are perhaps clearer about what loving our neighbour might mean, what might loving God look like? Or, more specifically, what might a dynamic relationship with God be like?

Imagine you're a fisherman, a professional, and you've been out on the lake all night, throwing out the nets, hauling them in – empty. Throwing out the nets, hauling them in – empty again. You're wet. And by four in the morning, even in the spring in Israel, you're cold. On the shore a hundred yards away, a man calls out, enquiring if you've caught anything. You tell him. And he tells you to throw your nets over the right side of the boat. It's dark, it's a hundred yards away and he couldn't possibly see a shoal of fish from there that you can't see from where you are standing in the boat, but you throw out the nets anyway – and you can't haul them in because they're too full. You make your way to shore.

The night has ended better than you could have imagined, but you're still wet and cold and no doubt hungry. But there are fish to haul in, count and distribute to the crew, the boats to beach, the nets to hang and the journey home to complete before you'll get anything warm in your belly.

But there on the beach you can see a wood fire glowing

orange and yellow in the dark, and wispy spirals of smoke and steam rising into the cold night air. And you can hear the sizzle of fish oil as it drips into the fire and the occasional sharp crackle as a flame leaps up and singes the fish's skin ... and the man says, 'Come and have breakfast.'

You weren't expecting him. He was dead, after all. But he's there anyway. Jesus, risen from the dead, with a myriad, myriad things he could be doing, a whole universe of places he could choose to manifest his bodily presence. But there he is, King of the universe, making breakfast on the beach for his friends after a long night's labour on the lake. Love is thoughtful. Love is practical. Love is hot grilled fish and bread, right there. And then.

And now?

We were both students. What they call in the UK 'mature' students, defined purely in terms of age, it should be noted. Over twenty-five. And recently married and, though certainly not poor, not exactly flush with cash. At the time, a local rather high-class store used to deliver a rather high-class selection of food that had reached its sell-by date to the college we were studying at. So, at the end of the day, the students who lived off campus, far, far away from the delights of college dining, would hover like seagulls behind a trawler, waiting for the day's catch. It was exam time and we were, I think, weary with revision. As I was about to leave home to join the circling seagulls, my wife said, 'I fancy some liver.' This, I hasten to add, is not a phrase often heard in Britain – liver not being a particularly popular dish. In fact, in all my time as a circling seagull, I couldn't remember a time when liver had arrived. It was

LOVE IS
THOUGHTFUL.
LOVE IS
PRACTICAL.
LOVE IS HOT
GRILLED FISH
AND BREAD.

as if she had asked for Galápagos Turtle. Still, I took off and the day's delivery arrived. There was steak and chicken and wonderful bread and fruit. The seagulls swooped and dived with all the elegance and politesse of a pack of jackals and came up clutching their trophies in their triumphant talons. 'Anyone want this?' came a voice. 'What is it?' 'Liver.' No one swooped, no one dived, no talon stretched out to grasp the package of burgundy flesh from the emptying crates. Except mine. Liver. Very fine calf liver and more than enough for two, though not quite enough for three.

It was the only day that the high-class store ever delivered liver.

A coincidence? Perhaps. But a gift, it seemed to us, from God. A gift, not even in response to a prayer, just in response to a preference. Love is thoughtful, love is practical. Love is hot grilled fish for a tired fisherman and succulent liver for a weary student, right there. Then and now.

And now? A few months ago, and a dear, dear friend is going through a terrible time. Bullied at work by a manager who knows how to put on a good show for her bosses but who harries, hassles, accuses those below her, breaks promises, sends out angry, accusatory emails like mortars into a housing estate – uncalled for, unnecessary, the kind of communications you might not believe if you hadn't seen them. Except with her favourites. Her favourites can do no wrong; her favourites are given credit for other people's work; her favourites are affirmed, protected, drawn round her to give the impression of more widespread popularity. My friend prays, seeks advice and seeks to address the issue in low-key ways. But the low-key ways fail – the examples of poor behaviour are so extreme they seem almost unbelievable. Eventually, she initiates a grievance procedure.

Someone in her home group senses that God is saying that she is like Esther, called to make a stand for such a time as this (Esther 4:14), not only for herself, but for others. Indeed, she is under no illusions: people who speak up are often put down. The barrage against her intensifies. As her friend, I am incensed. Actually I am incandescent with anger. One Sunday evening, having learned of an incident that would make *House of Cards* look like a game of snap, I couldn't sleep. After an hour or so, I went downstairs, sensing that I should read a passage that this morning's preacher had drawn our attention to. Actually, all day I'd been resisting the nudge to read it. I open it up. Isaiah 55.

And it hits me. This particular verse hits me:

Instead of the thorn-bush will grow the juniper, and instead of briers the myrtle will grow.
(ISAIAH 55:13)

I look it up in the Hebrew to check. Yes, the word for myrtle is 'hadassah'. And 'hadassah', apart from being the Hebrew for myrtle was Esther's name before she was given a Persian name. It's clear as a bell to me. A promise from God: myrtle/ Esther/my friend will flourish. And I knew it was for me – I'd studied Hebrew at Cambridge; I'd had cause to check the text of Esther just a couple of weeks previously; I'd found out that myrtle is a white star-shaped flower and that Esther meant 'star' in the Persian of the time. I'd heard about the house group's prayer … It was for me, God's reassurance to me about my dear, dear friend. I went straight to bed and fell asleep faster than you can say 'for such a time as this'.

Looking back, you can see God's tenderness, thoughtfulness, awareness of my circumstances, awareness of what I'd been reading, God leading me to that passage. The Bible is not just a means God uses to say general things that apply to all people; it is one of his means, by his Spirit, of saying very specific things to us as individuals that relate to our very specific circumstances – God's love is infinite and specific.

We know that about love. Love buys tickets for a band you adore – even if it puts them to sleep. Love puts a chocolate on the desk, the kind of chocolate you like – Swiss, smooth, milky with whole hazelnuts. Love dashes out to get you a sandwich when you don't have time – hummus on dark rye bread with sliced tomatoes and freshly milled black pepper. Love cuts out the article you might have missed, puts out the trash, prays that your friend will call when you're down …

Love bids you welcome … invites … offers.

Love listens.

Love banishes the fear of being known and rejected. Love rebukes because love wants the best for you. Love corrects you to raise you up, not to put you down; to liberate, not to imprison; to free, not to suppress the real you, the possible you, the fruitful you.

Love does not pacify, love empowers. Love coaxes the bud into bloom.

Love takes risks, asks for a rendezvous that you may reject, makes an offer that you may refuse, proffers a gift you may return. Love never compels.

Love sits with you in pain and exclusion, gives you time when your mind no longer knows what time is or who you are. Love makes sure your hair is well cut even when only the sick are there to see it. Love hides you under the table from Nazis, as Corrie ten Boom hid a Jew; love volunteers to take your place in Auschwitz's starvation chamber, as Saint Maximilian Kolbe did; love does not exact revenge against you, but walks the long road to reconciliation as Nelson Mandela did; love lays down their very life for you – as Jesus, son of Joseph, did.

Love will wait to give, but love's waiting is active ... it never stops yearning for union.

Love wants your love.

> *All night long on my bed*
> *I looked for the one my heart loves;*
> *I looked for him but did not find him.*
> *I will get up now and go about the city,*
> *through its streets and squares;*
> *I will search for the one my heart loves.*
> SONG OF SONGS 3:1–2

Love takes the initiative, makes an offer you can refuse ...

God is love.

Yes, God is love. This is therefore the element of all elements. And so it can find, and should find, expression in any context – work and home, sanctuary and supermarket, factory and field, bedroom and boardroom – at root it is about seeking the best for others, putting their interests first: designing a form that is easy to fill in, or looking for a computer that a 70-year-old who's never seen a radio can figure out, or finding a way to see a mental health specialist that's fast enough to prevent things getting worse, or creating a school menu that's nutritious, delicious and enough. Love is other-focused. And so those who love find themselves being other-focused even when there's no particular depth to the relationship, no sentiment, or direct emotional connection or actually any likelihood of it.

Shona worked in a bank. A big bank. Big banks, whatever the individual qualities of the vast majority of their staff, have not, in recent years, been swiftly associated with the word 'love'.

Selfishness? Greed? Intellectual arrogance?

Yes.

But not love.

Shona and the head office team she worked with had been charged with trimming costs in the retail banking division. They looked over their budgets and began to wield scalpel and axe. Shona enquired about a £1.5 billion write-off. 'That's bad consumer debts,' she was told. 'We can't do anything about those. Let's move on. They won't pay that back.'

Shona wondered.

She decided to meet some people in serious debt and make a short film to show the senior team how they really felt about their situation. She had a conviction that lots of people in debt don't want to be, didn't intend to be, feel shame, and actually want to pay people back. The film demonstrated that. How then to develop a better way of helping them? At the time, the bank allowed their call centre operators 7.5

minutes to talk to badly indebted customers. She suggested removing the targets so that the staff could really help them. 'But,' came the response, 'if we give the operators an hour they'll just talk about football and fashion.'

Shona wondered.

'Well, maybe some will. But I think most of our people want to do a good job, don't they?' (And for those who don't, she thought to herself, that is an issue for their manager, not one around which the whole system should be designed.) And so she developed new telephone protocols to help customers who were in trouble.

The estimated return for the bank over three years was £500 million pounds. Not small change. And the inestimable result for thousands of their customers was a clearer plan forward, a much better financial position, less debt, less distress, less shame, less guilt – and that wonderful sense of liberation and cleanness that comes from being able to honour your commitments.

And all that happened because one woman in a team in a huge bank saw things differently. But why was she able to see things differently? It wasn't that she had completed a PhD on the theology of banking or that her pastor had just finished a series of ten sermons on the ethics of financial services.

She saw the opportunity because she had a different attitude to people. Yes, all people have sinned but that doesn't mean that human beings created in the image of God don't also desire to do good, don't want to honour their commitments, don't want to 'love their neighbour' by paying them back. Shona knew that there is good in people to summon, not just evil to restrain.

She saw the opportunity because she saw the bank's call centre employees differently than the other managers. She had a biblical view of people. Yes, there is a propensity to laziness in most of us, an inclination to take the easy route. Most people, however, want to do a good job, most people enjoy doing a good job, and most people really enjoy helping others – it's a way of seeking their best, of putting their interests first, of 'loving' them.

She saw the opportunity because she had a biblical, not a cynical, view of people. She had a different doctrine of human nature, a biblical view that was neither rosily optimistic, nor glumly pessimistic. In *Prince Caspian*, C. S. Lewis captures something of the paradox of our human nature in Aslan's response to the prince's yearning to come of a more honourable lineage:

> *'You come of the Lord Adam and the Lady Eve and*
> *that is both honour enough to erect the head of*
> *the poorest beggar, and shame enough to bow the*
> *shoulders of the greatest emperor on earth.'*[27]

Shona was good at her job and her colleagues were too. It wasn't her superior professional competence that enabled her to make such a significant commercial contribution to the bank's bottom line and to the well-being of thousands of people. It was her gospel view of people. She was so infused with gospel truth and wisdom that she instinctively rejected the prevailing view of indebted customers, and didn't accept that nothing could be done with them or for them. She was

27 C. S. Lewis, *Prince Caspian (The Chronicles of Narnia)* (HarperCollinsChildren'sBooks, 2014).

not conformed to the thinking of the world around her, but had been transformed by the renewal of her mind (cf. Romans 12:2). And that's why she was able to make a transformative difference. Love, then, is a lens through which to look at the world, as well as a power to generate a caring response. True love is a settled determination to do the very best you can for other people – it's not just about rose petals on the pillow, it's about reducing the salt in our crisps, the waiting time in our hospitals, the distortions in our news.

And this is one of the ways God's people contribute to the *shalom* of our nation. We contribute not only through wonderful charitable initiatives like Christians against Poverty, but also more broadly by bringing the eternal, grace-drenched wisdom of Christ into the mainstream of our society, into the diverse places we find ourselves and into the many, many decisions we make daily. And we do so for the benefit of all and to the glory of God. May it be so.

And so it is that God the Father, out of his desire for relationship, for union with us, sends his willing Son to die on the cross.

The Great Commandment in Action

On the cross we glimpse the depth of what loving God and loving neighbour might have meant to Jesus. For Jesus, loving God with all his mind, heart, soul and strength meant agreeing to go through terrible pain to do God's will. Loving his neighbour as himself meant going through terrible pain so that all humankind might have a relationship with God the Father, as Jesus does.

Indeed, Jesus' loving initiative not only opens the way to restoring our relationship with him to the level of the uninhibited intimacy that was experienced in Eden, it creates an even more amazing possibility – a relationship of the intimacy that Jesus describes in John 17:

> *'My prayer is not for them alone. I pray also for those*
> *who will believe in me through their message, that all*
> *of them may be one, Father, just as you are in me and*
> *I am in you. May they also be in us so that the world*
> *may believe that you have sent me. I have given them*
> *the glory that you gave me, that they may be one as*
> *we are one – I in them and you in me.'*
> (vv.20–23)

This does not cease with mortal life but continues into immortal life where the prayer finds its ultimate fulfilment. From relational rupture in the garden of Eden to relational rapture for eternity, God's love is forever love.

Nevertheless, this relationship is not for its own sake. Jesus is, after all, sending his disciples into the world to change it. Unity with God is the prerequisite for effective engagement in the world and the essential resource for it.

Still, we're created not only with a desire to make a difference but with a yearning for a love that will last forever. That's why so many love songs sing of eternal love, 'always love', 'endless love', of love that 'is all around' for which there's 'no beginning' and 'no end'.

Yes, the intimacy of a satisfying marriage is a joy indeed and celebrated in the Bible with love poetry that beautifully melds the romantic and the sexual:

Let my beloved come into his garden
and taste its choice fruits.
SONG OF SONGS 4:16

But even that cannot meet the need for the kind of forever love humans are created for.

No, as Jesus' prayer clarifies, those who follow him are in the Father as he is in the Father and will in eternity know the perfection of intimacy. However, such intimacy doesn't mean we lose our identity. We don't drown in God's love but soar on its wings.

Intimacy and Individuality

When we die, we will not evanesce into unconscious nothingness within the Godhead, as in Hinduism, nor undergo a Pullmanesque molecular merging with nature. Rather, our unique God-created identity will be preserved. Just as the identity of Jesus, God the Son, remains distinct from his Father's identity even though they are intimately and inextricably connected, so we as human beings retain our individuality. Indeed, in the new heaven and the new earth, even though we will have new bodies, we will be recognizable as the same person we were.

The purpose of Jesus' self-giving on the cross was therefore not only so that the penalty for human rebellion would be paid off, nor that people would be ransomed out of the dominion of darkness – though Jesus did pay that penalty and people are rescued from living under Satan's malicious rule. No, the ultimate purpose of Jesus' self-sacrifice was so that we might enjoy an uninhibited, eternal, transformative, satisfying, intimate relationship with the triune God. Tyndale, the first translator of the Bible into English, coined the word 'atonement', 'at-one-ment', to capture this idea. Through Jesus' sacrifice we are 'at-oned' with him.

Indeed, though there are few things sweeter than being forgiven, the yearning of the human heart is not primarily to be told that we are forgiven but for the restored relationship that forgiveness creates.

We want more than legal absolution, or a clean record, or an official pardon; we yearn for the ease, the openness that was there before – the sweetness and relief of embrace, now that the hurt and anger and guilt have been swept away. Of course, in human marriage, this may express itself in sex, and some say that 'make-up sex' is the best kind. But even in sex the abiding memory may not be of the particular intensity of the physical pleasure but of the look of love on the beloved's face as it is given. We yearn for restored union.

This idea of closeness was inherent in the early sacrificial system that God instituted. Indeed, one of the key words for sacrifice used in the book of Leviticus is *karav*. And the root meaning of *karav* is 'close', 'near'. So to bring an offering to the altar is in Hebrew *yakriv karav* ... 'to bring close a closener'. In the New Testament, the theme of closeness is expanded. We read that after Jesus died on the cross, the veil that used to cover the entrance to the Holy of Holies in the temple, the place that only one chosen priest could enter and only on the Day of Atonement, was torn in two from top to bottom by God.

Open Access

The implication of this is clear: the way to God is open at all times for all people. The writer to the Hebrews makes the same point. Because of what Jesus has done we can

> *approach God's throne of grace with confidence, so that we may receive mercy and find grace to help us in our time of need.*
> HEBREWS 4:16

The closeness that Jesus envisages is not primarily about physical proximity, like getting close to a famous person. Nor is it primarily about physical touch, like the physical touch that John the disciple would have experienced when leaning on Jesus' chest at the Last Supper (John 13:23). The closeness that Jesus envisages is not in 'space' – he hasn't simply moved into the neighbourhood or the spare room or sat down at the kitchen table – no, the closeness Jesus envisages is in our very 'being'. Jesus has moved into our inner being by his Spirit. Indeed, on the eve of his death, he tells his disciples that it is better for them that he goes away physically:

> 'But very truly I tell you, it is for your good that I am going away. Unless I go away, the Advocate will not come to you; but if I go, I will send him to you.'
> JOHN 16:7

This Advocate, as John makes clear, is the Holy Spirit, the third person of the Trinity, who will dwell inside the disciples and will teach, guide and strengthen them. This divine presence, the inner assurance of God's love and constancy, is their source of peace, their *shalom* – whatever the world throws at them. So God's desired relationship with us is not mere closeness, he is not merely 'there', not just 'with' us, like an accompanying angel, he is 'within' us.

And because of this we do not need to visit a building to pray to God or set aside special times to talk to him. There is always access. That's why the apostle Paul can encourage Christians to 'pray continually' (1 Thessalonians 5:17).

Prayer is not dial-up, it's 4G.

It isn't a call to a secluded life in a monastery, a convent, or a lonely hut on some bleak and wuthering height, but a reminder that God is in us by his Spirit, that we have open access to communing with him at all times – in offices and factories, kitchens and schoolrooms, in sickness and bombardment, and in the valley of the shadow of death.

So, for example, one Western business person returning from serving the people in a Third World slum, said, 'I have never experienced such a sense of the presence of God in my life, as I did when I was in that place.' And he said this in an adult Sunday school class in a rich suburb. That, of course, is not to say that other Western business people don't experience God's presence in their ordinary everyday work in the affluent West. One man put it this way to me: 'When I work at my company, I feel God's pleasure.'

And so we can see here how the five relational factors we looked at earlier – directness, continuity, multiplexity, parity, and commonality of purpose – might apply not only to our relationships with people but with God.

PRAYER
IS NOT
DIAL-UP,
IT'S 4G.

The God Who Is There

Firstly, we need *directness* of contact. We don't just want to read about God or hear stories of what he's been up to in other countries or in other people's lives; we yearn to hear from him ourselves, to know his presence ourselves. That requires time set aside for him – as a married couple might set aside time just for each other even though they have nineteen children, five dogs and an aardvark. However, it also, and sometimes more challengingly, requires a greater consciousness of God in our everyday tasks and encounters. Just as the warmth and attention of a host can transform a simple meal of beans on toast into something that feels as lavish as a feast, and you as honoured as royalty, so inviting God into our ordinary, everyday lives opens the way for us to see how he might touch and transform the ordinary with the fragrance of beyond.

The God Who Doesn't Leave

Secondly, our relationship with God is enhanced over time – with *continuity*. The longer we're with him and conscious of him being with us, the deeper our trust and delight can grow. It is not just that with hindsight you can see more of the ways he has rescued you, provided for you, been there. It's not just, in my case, that I have become more and more convinced that his wisdom is simply better than anything on offer anywhere, in any era, that his ways are simply the best, and the only road to a freedom that is genuinely liberating. Rather, it's that the longer you walk with him and talk with him, the more you know what he's like, the more you know that whatever the circumstances he can still surprise you, he can still answer the question: 'How are you going to make something of this mess, in entirely unpredictable but gracious ways?' As with the deepest friendships, there's always more to discover. The mystery of his majesty, and yet his readiness to come close to us, deepens in wonder and gratitude.

The God Involved in All

Thirdly, our relationship with God is enriched through *multiplexity*. Through knowing him and seeing him at work in a variety of different contexts and situations, we grow in love of who he is. When he answers prayer for a difficult client meeting (he did), when he restores a lost, very old, literally irreplaceable iron key in response to a child's heartfelt prayer (he did), when his presence is palpable in an Alzheimer sufferer's moment of clarity as a son comes to say 'goodbye' (it was) – through such experiences our love and appreciation for God grows.

The God with an Open Ear

Fourthly, there is *parity of power*, but of a particular kind. Of course, no human being is equal to God in any area of competence or power, and yet every human being is valued. Indeed, we see in God's relationships with people that he wants to hear from us, that we have a voice, that Abraham can 'negotiate' with God over the destruction of Sodom (Genesis 18), that the psalmist can cry out in protest at God's apparent indifference (e.g. Psalm 22), that Jesus, perfect in obedience to his Father, can ask if there is another way other than the torture of the cross (Luke

22:42). Furthermore, whilst God could accomplish all that he wishes to accomplish on his own, he chooses to do a great deal of it in cooperation with human beings. We matter in his purposes.

The God of Adventure

Fifthly, the disciples of Christ share a *commonality of purpose* with God. He has invited us to join with him in changing the world, in caring for the sick, in changing world trade agreements so that the poor are fed and the enslaved liberated, and in modelling ways of living that put people before things, time before money, love before logos, generosity before rights, Christ the Son of God before King Konsummon, son of Mammon.

The Christian, every Christian, is called to be yeast, leaven, an agent of transformation in God's mission of transforming, reconciling and restoring the whole universe. This is the great adventure God calls people to be part of, and the result is that the everyday is tinged with the eternal, the routine with the fragrance of forever, the chore with the possibility of being a conduit of love and a channel of his eternal grace.

Indeed, the word 'grace' in the New Testament is used in two quite distinct ways. Firstly, it means 'undeserved favour' and is used to describe the reality that those who come into relationship with Christ (and therefore enjoy all the benefits of being his children) do not do so through any merit of their own or because of anything that they have done. You can't buy your way into heaven or get into heaven because of wondrous acts of charity, extraordinary beauty or good citizenship. It is a free gift of God – undeserved by anyone.

Secondly, grace is used to describe God's 'empowering presence'. So it is that in every single one of his letters, Paul addresses Christians with the words, 'Grace and peace to you'. Since they are all already believers, what Paul is praying for is God's empowering presence with and within them, the grace that enables them to do what God wants them to do, to be who he is calling them to be – whatever the circumstances. Again, this is essentially a relational promise – I'll be there. In power.

We can know his presence – on occasion, almost tangibly – as we do things he wants done, not simply as we speak and listen. Indeed, this reflects the reality that in human relationships, bonds of closeness are not just forged through verbal communication but through the communion-building impact of shared tasks and activities. Somebody can be 'known' deeply through their actions and a lasting bond forged without words. Working on a shared challenge can create a depth of respect and commitment out of all proportion to the verbal intimacy shared.

Indeed, the wonder of the God revealed in the Bible, and known in my experience, is that he loves 'me', not only in all my faults, rebellions and weaknesses but in particular ways that make his love real to me – like someone who knows that their loved one's favourite flower is not a rose, or a lily, or an iris, but a daffodil, which was my aunt's favourite flower.

And so it was with daffodils, not roses or lilies or irises, that my mother adorned my aunt's coffin.

And in no less tender and personal ways does our God know and love us.

*Happiness is
when what you think,
what you say,
and what you do
are in harmony.*
MAHATMA GANDHI

*We love because he
first loved us.*
THE APOSTLE JOHN

*The love of the fellowship of the church
was overwhelming ... and I said to myself,
'These are people that are godly.'
Yes, they have faults like everyone else
as a church, but I was overwhelmed
by the help they gave my wife,
bringing food to her. They didn't know her,
and that just consolidated the faith I had,
and still does to this day.*
QUOTED IN JOURNEYS AND STORIES,
BY NICK SPENCER AND PETER NEILSON

CHAPTER 7

LOVING TOGETHER

or

COMMUNITIES THAT GIVE IT A GO

I don't think anyone ever graduates from the school of love.

Every day I seem to crash up against the limits of my own capacity to respond selflessly and generously to people around me – if not always in deed, then certainly in thought. The horizons of my heart need expanding. But I learn from others and I see it in others. And Jesus wants others to see it in us, particularly in the community of his church. As Jesus himself said:

> '*A new command I give you: love one another. As I have loved you, so you must love one another. By this everyone will know that you are my disciples, if you love one another.*'
> JOHN 13:34–35

We'll come back to this, but it's important to note here that Jesus doesn't say people will know you are my disciples by your love for strangers, though the community of Christ is clearly commanded to show hospitality to strangers, to seek to meet the needs of the poor and the sick in their communities. Indeed, historically the reason, humanly speaking, that Christianity grew was not just because it was true but because it was good news for people's lives and therefore attractive to believers and not-yet believers.

In the much acclaimed *The Rise of Christianity*[28] historian Rodney Stark points out how the response of Christians to social conditions and historic events in the first two centuries after Christ made it compellingly good news for others. In a Roman Empire that practised infanticide of girls and oppressed women through enforced and highly dangerous abortions, the Christian stance against infanticide and abortion was good news for women.

Similarly, when the Roman Empire was hit by terrible epidemics in AD 165 and 251, overall the pagan population neither looked after those who shared their beliefs, nor those who didn't. However, the combination of Christian teaching about heaven and about loving your neighbour meant that Christians nursed sick Christians and sick pagans. Independent of any miraculous intervention, the survival rate was higher among Christians and their pagan friends than amongst those who were not connected to Christians. The gospel was good news for the sick. And this stemmed from Christian doctrines. Beliefs drove actions and offered a highly benevolent alternative to the prevailing culture.

Stark summarizes it:

> *Christianity revitalised life in Greco-Roman cities*
> *(hugely overcrowded, disease-ridden places for*
> *the most part) by providing new norms and new*

28 Rodney Stark, *The Rise of Christianity: How the Obscure, Marginal, Jesus Movement Became the Dominant Religious Force in the Western World in a Few Centuries* (Princeton, N.J.: Princeton University Press, 1996; New York: HarperCollins, 1997).

*relationships. To cities filled with the homeless
and impoverished, Christianity offered charity as
well as hope. To cities filled with newcomers and
strangers, Christianity offered an immediate basis for
attachments. To cities filled with orphans and widows,
Christianity provided a new and extended sense of
family. To cities torn by ethnic strife, Christianity
offered a new basis for social solidarity. And to
cities faced with epidemics, fires, and earthquakes,
Christianity offered effective nursing services.[29]*

Interestingly, this capacity of Christian communities to offer attractive responses to broad societal problems found contemporary endorsement from Matthew Parris, one of *The Times'* leading commentators. His travels in the ravaged continent of Africa led him to this conclusion:

*Now a confirmed atheist, I've become convinced of
the enormous contribution that Christian evangelism
makes in Africa: sharply distinct from the work of secular
NGOs, government projects and international aid efforts.
These alone will not do. Education and training alone
will not do. In Africa Christianity changes people's hearts.
It brings a spiritual transformation. The rebirth is real.
The change is good [...]*

*Those who want Africa to walk tall amid 21st-century
global competition must not kid themselves that
providing the material means or even the knowhow*

---

29 Stark, *Rise of Christianity*, 161.

that accompanies what we call development will
make the change. A whole belief system must first be
supplanted.[30]

Parris has not yet come to the conclusion that Christianity is probably, or even possibly, the best idea in the world, but he's certainly convinced it's the best idea for Africa. It's a start.

Closer to home, Roy Hattersley, historian, biographer, former Member of Parliament and self-avowed atheist, wrote in *The Guardian*: 'We have to accept that most believers are better human beings.'[31]

By which he meant that believers simply do much more for the sick, the poor, the disadvantaged – even if they don't share their faith – than atheists. And he has the data to prove it:

Civilised people do not believe that drug addiction
and male prostitution offend against divine
ordinance. But those who do are the men and women
most willing to change the fetid bandages, replace the
sodden sleeping bags and – probably most difficult of
all – argue, without a trace of impatience, that the
time has come for some serious medical treatment.
Good works, John Wesley insisted, are no guarantee
of a place in heaven. But they are most likely to be
performed by people who believe that heaven exists.

---

30 Matthew Parris, 'As an atheist, I truly believe Africa needs God', *The Times*, 27 December 2009. https://www.thetimes.co.uk/article/as-an-atheist-i-truly-believe-africa-needs-god-3xj9bm80h8m .

31 Roy Hattersley, Faith does breed charity', *The Guardian*, 12 September 2005. https://www.theguardian.com/world/2005/sep/12/religion.uk .

The correlation is so clear that it is impossible to
doubt that faith and charity go hand in hand.[32]

By contrast, other secular thinkers, like, for example, the UK's former Culture Secretary Chris Smith, believe that we can recover our kindness as a society without recourse to the well from which it sprang – relationship with a loving Creator. He wants the grapes without the vine.

History and common sense reveal that it can't be done. Whatever the failings of the church – and there have been many, in many countries, across many centuries – none of them obviate the reality that where Gospel doctrines take hold, societies are much, much more likely to flourish.

The Limits of Our Love

If our national well-being cannot be fully realized without God, might it also be true on a personal level? Do we have the capacity to love our neighbour as we would want?

Are we able, without divine help, to love the stranger, the alien, the person so much poorer than us, the person so much richer? Douglas Coupland, not himself a person of Christian faith, put it this way in the mouth of one of his characters in his novel *Life after God*:

My secret is that I need God – that I am sick and
can no longer make it alone. I need God to help me
give, because I no longer seem to be capable of giving;
to help me to be kind, as I no longer seem capable of

---

32 Ibid.

*kindness; to help me love, as I seem beyond being able
to love.*[33]

How much space do we have in our hearts for others? Can
we love as we would love to love without God?

Is it easy to love selflessly, to set aside our own agendas,
to quench the oceanic thirst of our egos? Is it easy to die to
the insistent demands of me, myself and I? To genuinely
and consistently put others first?

Don't most of us need help to do that?

And how does being in relationship with God help us?

Firstly, human beings are not only designed to love; we
are designed to know God's love. When we don't, there
will always be an underlying sense of dissatisfaction, of
restlessness.

Being loved by God fills the need for him that he has
created. Furthermore, it is the soul-deep knowledge of being
totally loved and accepted by the most important person in
the universe that liberates us from our debilitating concerns
about ourselves. *He* loves me – and frees me to love more
and more like him – and helps me by his Spirit.

The Antidote to Fear

As we saw in chapter two, fear is one of the great inhibitors in
most people's lives – fear of failure, fear of embarrassment,
fear of looking odd, fear of death … Fear paralyses action,
crushes initiative, makes us look away rather than look
ahead, look down rather than look up. Fear is the enemy.

---

33 Douglas Coupland, *Life after God* (New York: Simon & Schuster, 1994), 359.

HUMAN BEINGS
ARE NOT ONLY
DESIGNED TO
LOVE; WE ARE
DESIGNED TO
KNOW GOD'S
LOVE.

We know from psychological research that, overall, children who have been raised by loving parents in a secure, stable environment are more likely to be courageous, more likely to take risks, and more likely to swim against the popular tide. Love creates a foundation of security that acts both like a springboard and a parachute. Simultaneously, the experience of being loved launches people into adventures that the fearful would not contemplate and catches them when they otherwise might come down to earth with too great a bump.

But suppose we didn't grow up in such a nurturing environment? Are we doomed to be ruled by fear? And even if we did, does human love remove all fear? Does it on its own satisfy the human yearning for eternity, for the love that will never die? Can it remove the fear of death? Or reassure us that our everyday, ordinary lives are actually significant in the grand scheme of things?

No, ultimately, only the perfect love that we can experience in relationship with God can drive out the fear that prevents us from fully giving ourselves to others. For to truly love another person is not to need their love in return in order to carry on loving. We may desire their love, but if we need it, then our love will be tinged with selfishness or fear that the love we need will not be given. If, on the other hand, I know that I am totally loved by God, I don't 'need' anyone else's love to keep loving. As the Apostle John put it in one of his letters to a community of Christians: 'Perfect love drives out fear', and 'We love because he first loved us' (1 John 4:18, 19). The experience of God's transforming love empowers us to love in ways that would otherwise be entirely beyond us. The paradox of love is this: our grasp of our own infinite value and specialness to God does not make us self-focused but makes us forget ourselves and orient ourselves to others. Love liberates us from ourselves by assuring us of our value.

So it is no accident that Jesus links loving God with loving neighbour. Ultimately, neither can be fulfilled without the other.

Loving beyond Our Means

A while back, a man looked me in the eye and told me that his wife didn't love him, like him, desire him, appreciate him or respect him. That doesn't leave much out.

What kept him from bitterness? What kept him from seeking comfort elsewhere?

What enabled him to carry on, standing by her, trying to love her when nothing came back except rejection? To carry on offering the kiss when the kiss was not returned, when she might turn a cheek but never offer her lips? What kept bitterness from taking root even if from time to time it tainted his tongue? For him, it was the sense of being loved by God, that he was fundamentally OK. God had lined the walls of the man's heart with the reality of his love, and that worked to repel the thoughts of worthlessness and the impact of rejection.

God's command to love does not come without the resources to fulfill it. We cannot fully love God without his help. And we cannot truly, freely, wholeheartedly, selflessly love our neighbour without being in relationship with the God of love, who not only shows us what love should look like but empowers us by his Spirit to love beyond our means. Indeed, it is God's provision of his Spirit that makes growing in our capacity to love possible. If it weren't for God's Spirit, strengthening and renewing us, the Christian life would be one long, joyless uphill struggle of the will to love in ways that are utterly beyond our natural capacities.

Biblically, it is only by being in Christ that we can love in his ways. Jesus puts it this way: 'I am the vine; you are the branches' (John 15:5). The branches can produce no fruit unless they are in the vine, cannot love as he would have us love if we are cut off from the source of that love. Abide in the vine, and the Spirit he sends flows.

And we need it because the one we are to imitate sets a high bar that would be impossible to attain without his help. In one of his letters, John the disciple put it like this:

> *This is how we know what love is: Jesus Christ laid*
> *down his life for us. And we ought to lay down*
> *our lives for our brothers and sisters. If anyone has*
> *material possessions and sees a brother or sister in*
> *need but has no pity on them, how can the love of*
> *God be in that person? Dear children, let us not love*
> *with words or speech but with actions and in truth.*
> *This is how we know that we belong to the truth and*
> *how we set our hearts at rest in his presence.*
> 1 JOHN 3:16–19

This, however, is not just an individual response. Those who follow the triune relational God are summoned to be in a community that is a model of purposeful loving relationships and a fountain of unconditional love.

Do we so love one another in the church that people know that we are Jesus' disciples?

The Community That Gives It a Go

The church is the representative community of the triune God on earth. Our relationships of humble, purposeful, open, vulnerable love are intended to mirror the loving relationships within the Trinity. Indeed, throughout the Bible we see that, though God does call individuals to love and obey him, his desire is to make a people, to create a community. So he doesn't just create Adam, he creates male and female and calls on them to multiply. Similarly, he calls Abraham so that through him a people, a community, might grow. Furthermore, when someone becomes a follower of Jesus, is 'born again' as Jesus puts it, they are not born again into splendid isolation, not simply changed into an individual who now relates in a different way to God and to the people they encounter along the way. No, the person who is 'born again' is born again into a new community, a new family. Indeed, in the New Testament, the antidote to loneliness is not to find a partner but to find a community.

The church ought to be the best place to be single in.

Yours may not be, but that does not obviate the truth that it is meant to be. And could be. Indeed, maturity in Christ cannot be achieved by an individual on their own because it is in the community of God's people that wisdom is found. The church is a body that needs all its parts functioning to be whole. And so the quality of relationships within the church is vital. After all, if Jesus' kind of selfless love doesn't bloom in the people who claim to follow him, maybe he hasn't really provided the resources, the power, to live it.

Well, what is the quality of relationships in the church you are part of?

Probably quite friendly. But there is a world of difference between friendliness and friendship, between affability and a determined, humble commitment to seek the best for other people. There is a world of difference between being able to chat away about current affairs or *Strictly* or *Star Wars* and the courageous capacity to be authentic and vulnerable with other people, to risk admitting failure, weakness, sin, need, pain and so pave a path to being truly known, accepted, strengthened, healed.

The Joy of Generous Living

Similarly, there is a world of difference between communities that meet and greet on a Sunday and communities that serve to foster the kinds of relationships that genuinely support one another during the week – communities that pray for the fruitfulness of the cabbies and cleaners and corporate execs among them; communities that make meals for couples who've just had a child (as some do); communities that don't just pray when your pipes burst but scramble into action and come round, ready to mop and dry, to replaster and repaint (as some have). People who put their time and talent and treasure where their heart is. People who notice that your smallish car is ten years old,

THERE IS A
WORLD OF
DIFFERENCE
BETWEEN
FRIENDLINESS
AND
FRIENDSHIP.

has only two doors and one front seat that doesn't fold forward anymore, that you already have two children, and that your wife is heavily pregnant with your third, who help you buy a replacement (as one couple did for my family). People who come into your workplace and pray for you, the work, your co-workers and the organization. People who, when they discover that your wife has to spend a month in hospital before the birth of your third child, offer to pick up your other two children from school and take them to the hospital to see their mother for a couple of hours before the father gets home – as a member of our church did.

What was in it for them?

The joy of living in God's generous ways.

It is indeed more blessed to give than to receive, though I do love presents, nice notes, small amounts of chocolate, wooden toys, kisses, hugs, surprise visits … When we give, we enter into God's generous giving nature. Love gives – expecting nothing in return. And this kind of love is one of the primary ways in which people who don't know Jesus will know that Christians are his disciples – apprentices of this particular master – through our love for one another.

The disciple is therefore not primarily someone who knows the Bible, though they may, or someone who goes to a church building on a Sunday, though they probably will; a disciple of Jesus is someone who loves those who love Jesus in a practical, intentional way. The way of the disciple is the way of selfless love. And one of the goals of the community of Christ is to help us love in this way in all of our life –

when we're together and when we're apart. Discipleship is essentially an adventure in learning to love.

Whilst the church as a whole may have a poor image, LICC (London Institute for Contemporary Christianity) research reveals that people's actual experience of the Christians they've met and the Christian communities they have experienced is far more positive. Indeed, the example of open, welcoming, caring communities on people's journey towards becoming followers of Jesus seems, if anything, to have grown in significance in the last twenty years. These communities may or may not have multimedia tech, espresso machines and a five-string bass guitarist, but people are often simply stunned by the practical, no-strings-attached love of the 'ordinary' people they meet and the ordinary-extraordinary ways in which love is expressed.

The representatives of Jesus are therefore to be characterized by the kind of generosity that eases pain, alleviates hunger, liberates from addictions, sets captives free, sets people on a road, seeks the best for people, and wants them to grow in love for God and in practical, humble love for one another.

This is not easily achieved.

The story goes, a true story I'm told, of a pastor going to another church to hear a friend speak. The sermon was all about the need to forgive each other, the need for forbearance and patience. The pastor went away concerned for his friend but delighted because there was no way that he needed to preach such a sermon in his own church. All was bud and blossom in his garden. But later in the day, it hit him like a hippo: the reason there was no need to preach a sermon on forgiveness, forbearance and patience in his church was because no one really knew each other well enough to be irritated by them. The relationships were gleamingly superficial. Safe, sanitized and achingly hollow.

Surface harmony may actually be a symptom of poor relationships and the absence of a challenging shared purpose. By contrast, arguments about how something might be achieved or an appropriate rebuke towards those who unnecessarily block progress are often indicators of healthy relationships amongst those who have a meaningful shared purpose.

The Countercultural Community

The kind of community the Bible envisages is one where the barriers that tend to exist between people of different race, age, gender, sexual orientation, socio-economic and educational categories, and even musical preferences, are broken down. In the Bible, we read that 'there is neither Jew nor Gentile, neither slave nor free, nor is there male and female, for you are all one in Christ Jesus' (Galatians 3:28). Historically, of course, the church's record has been mixed. But what is the situation in your community? Is there no male and female, no middle class and working class, no graduate or non-graduate, no white, no black, no Asian, no asylum seeker, no teenager or middle-aged? Have the barriers that our society tends to erect actually been torn down and replaced by a deeper reconciliation and love that transcends such categories? Is there any evidence of love for people not like 'us'? Is there any generosity for fellow

Christians where we don't live? Like the church in a North London suburb that, despite the heavy demands on its own (deficit) budget, still gives £10,000 a year to support the work of a church in one of the poorest areas in the UK. Or the people giving sacrificially of time and money to help orphans in Romania, refugees in Darfur and trafficked children all round the world.

Still, whatever the image of the church, the reality is that in the UK and in the US, no community does more voluntarily for people beyond their immediate family than Christians through churches in formal and informal ways – through youth work, breakfast clubs, homework clubs, social clubs, mums and toddlers, Saturday clubs for divorced fathers, chaplains in hospitals and prisons, counselling, marriage preparation, drug rehabilitation, work among prostitutes, the homeless, the homebound and the hungry, feeding programmes and food banks, CAP centres, Street Pastors, visiting the sick and elderly ...

And though this work is often done openly in the name of Jesus, it rarely requires any faith commitment to receive it. The Salvation Army, for example, does not ask homeless AIDS-infected drug addicts if they believe in Jesus before providing shelter, food, care and a drug rehabilitation programme.

This is not to say that more might not be done. Of course. But it is exhilarating to hear of the creativity and sacrifice of so many communities, and indeed the skill of so many ministers in mobilizing and empowering God's people to 'neighbour love' where they are.

If the church has historically been strong at loving one

another in physical, emotional, financial and spiritual crisis, we've been less strong at loving one another in the challenges that many face out in the hustle and bustle of our Monday to Saturday lives beyond the church. On the whole, church communities have spent much less time, money, energy, study, and prayer enabling Christians to be agents of *shalom* in workplaces, at the school gate, in the gym, down the pub. Similarly, we've put much less energy into providing wisdom for ordinary daily ministry and witness, or for the common challenges of life – studying, choosing a life partner, choosing a job, parenting children, creating a nurturing home, dealing with ageing or sick parents, working under time pressure and ethical pressure ... But discipleship is for all of life. And the core task of the church is to make disciples.

That was Jesus' own focus in his three years of public ministry. And it was this task that he commanded his own disciples to pursue:

> *Therefore go and make disciples of all nations,*
> *baptising them in the name of the Father and of the*
> *Son and of the Holy Spirit, and teaching them to obey*
> *everything I have commanded you. And surely I am*
> *with you always, to the very end of the age.*
> MATTHEW 28:19–20

A disciple is not primarily a student seeking to acquire information but an active, intentional apprentice seeking to live their whole life in the way their master lives life, to be holy as God is holy in every aspect of their lives.

Jesus' Relational Way

When the disciples heard Jesus' command to make disciples, I wonder what they thought he meant? I suspect they thought he meant that they should go and have the kind of relationships with other people that he'd had with them – eating, travelling, teaching, listening, correcting, exposing character flaws to build character, identifying skills gaps to build their skills ... It was personal, it was close, it was open. And it was costly. So, loving one another as whole-life disciples means getting to know enough about each other's whole lives – the people we naturally meet, the places we normally go, the things we habitually do, the challenges we face, the opportunities we have – to pray knowledgably, advise wisely, and encourage astutely. How will people outside the church know that we follow Jesus? Particularly when most of them aren't coming to church? Yes, by experiencing and seeing godly generosity and kindness to those in need. And yes, by seeing his people so thoughtfully loved that they are empowered and equipped to live and love well, joyously and generously, in their daily frontline contexts, shining like stars in a culture that frazzles and dehumanizes so many of our fellow-citizens.

'You must sit down,' says Love, 'and taste my meat.'
GEORGE HERBERT, 'LOVE (III)'

CHAPTER 8

GOT A BETTER IDEA?

or

GIVE THIS ONE A TRY

Love God, love your neighbour. The best idea in the world?

Well, it may have seemed an absurd claim, an adman's claim, but has anyone in history ever come up with a better idea?

Has anyone in history come up with a better, more compelling piece of advice? Think about how what you do, think and say will affect your relationship with God and with others. Live your life in a way that builds your relationship with God and seeks the best for others. It's a piece of advice that addresses the deepest needs of the human spirit, the need to be released from our self-obsession and to find hope and significance and perfect love in a relationship with an eternal God that knows us intimately, always wants the best for us and will never, ever, not ever leave us or abandon us.

A forever love.

Love God, love your neighbour. An idea that is the litmus test for any other idea.

An idea not just with legs but with wings, an idea on which healthy friendships and healthy families and healthy companies and healthy churches and healthy societies can be built. A piece of advice that has the power to transform the world for the better. Which is why it's not just a recommendation from a consultant but a command from the Maker of the universe. It is, after all, *his* world.

And it's an idea that can be lived and is worth giving one's life to and one's life for. Indeed, as we look at what lies behind this idea, we get a glimpse of who God is – of the relentless, life-giving love God has for his world and for us, the astounding truth of how we can be part of the way he extends his love outwards to the people we meet and work with day by day. And we get a clearer understanding of the one who spoke those words, who walked his talk through the dusty streets of Jerusalem and out to Calvary hill.

Has anyone in the history of the world ever lived out their own advice with such sobering integrity?

Has anyone demonstrated the beauty and cost of that idea so wondrously?

Setting aside the glories and comforts of heaven for the ordinary life of a carpenter and the cruel death of a criminal.

Laying down his own life because he loved his Father so much, laying down his own life because he loved his neighbour so much.

Because he loves us so much.

Loves you. Loves me.

And will always be there. With us.

And has been.

And is.

May it be so for you.

TAKING RELATIONAL LIVING FURTHER

If you're interested in exploring relational living further, then both the London Institute for Contemporary Christianity (LICC) and the Jubilee Centre have websites with resources and articles on a wide range of topics, plus information on key books and links to other relevant websites.

Recommended Resources

GROUP REFLECTIONS

licc.org.uk/bestidea – 'The Great Commandments and Relational Living', Joe Warton and Christine Hughes. A group Bible study resource from LICC, keyed into (*Probably) the Best Idea in the World*.

jubilee-centre.org/BARC – Small group Bible study and discussion material on building better relationships in churches and communities, as well as a DIY audit called 'Building a Relational Church' are available.

WEBSITES

jubilee-centre.org – Explore if you're interested in the application of relational thinking to public policy issues, to business and corporate contexts, to the life of your local church and to a wide range of issues in private life.

The Jubilee Centre's sister organizations:

relationshipsfoundation.org – The Relationships Foundation.
relationalschools.org – Relational Schools Project.

relationalpeacebuilding.org – Relational Peacebuilding.
relationalthinking.net – Relational Thinking Network.
licc.org.uk – For a wide range of exercises, resources or
Bible studies that help you live fruitfully for Christ in your
Monday to Saturday contexts – as well as your Sunday –
and that help your church help others. You can also sign
up to receive LICC's punchy free biweekly short emails –
'Word for the Week' and 'Connecting with Culture'.

BOOKS
Free to Live, Guy Brandon (SPCK, 2010) – A lifestyle
book that explores relationships as the key to freedom
and well-being. A free small group study guide can be
downloaded from jubilee-centre.org/free-to-live.
The Relational Manager, Michael Schluter and David
John Lee (Lion Hudson, 2009) – Sets out strategies for
transforming your workplace and your life through putting
relationships first.
*Jubilee Manifesto: A Framework, Agenda & Strategy for
Christian Social Reform*, edited by Michael Schluter and John
Ashcroft (IVP, 2005) – A detailed study of biblical teaching
about major policy areas such as welfare, economics and
criminal justice, with a view to understanding what a
relational society looks like in practice and how we can go
about influencing our society.
Fruitfulness on the Frontline, Mark Greene (IVP, 2017)
– Brimming with real-life stories, biblical insight and
practical steps, this spirit-lifting, horizon-expanding book
opens up fresh vistas on making a significant and multi-
faceted impact for Christ in our everyday contexts – work,

school gate, gym, supermarket … to the glory of God.

Imagine Church: Releasing Whole-Life Disciples, Neil Hudson, (IVP, 2012) – Groundbreaking book on how 'ordinary' churches can become richly relational communities that help one another live out their whole lives – at home, work, church, in the neighbourhood – as followers of Jesus in his mission in the world.

About the Jubilee Centre

The Jubilee Centre is a research and policy think tank that offers a biblical perspective on social, economic and political issues, and equips Christians to be salt and light in the public square. This is carried out through research, training and events in Cambridge and across the UK. Subscribe online for free to receive 'Cambridge Papers' and 'Engage' each quarter. For more information, call or email:

T: 01223 566319
E: *info@jubilee-centre.org*
W: *jubilee-centre.org*
Facebook.com/JubileeCentre
@JubileeCentre

About The London Institute for Contemporary Christianity

What difference does following Jesus make to our ordinary daily lives, to the things we normally do, in the places we normally spend time, with the people we usually meet? How can we live fruitfully and faithfully, sharing and showing the love and wisdom and ways of Christ right where we are?

Back in 1982, LICC was founded to answer that question by one of the most influential Bible teachers and Christian leaders of the 20th century – John Stott. He and his co-founders wanted to change the story of the church in the UK and globally – change it to a story of God's people envisioned, empowered, encouraged. God's people sent into their daily contexts, confident in him, in the necessity and beauty of his plan of salvation, and in his call to join in his transformative purposes for every nook of his world. Today the team at LICC works with Christians and leaders from across the denominations. Their aim is to help Christians make a difference for Christ out on their daily frontlines, to help church leaders help them, and to help theological educators train church leaders for this central calling of Christ to make fruitful whole-life disciples for the whole of life – for the blessing of our nation and the salvation of many.

W: licc.org.uk
T: 020 7399 9555
E: *mail@licc.org.uk*
 Facebook.com/LICCLtd
 @LICCLtd

ABOUT THE AUTHOR

Mark Greene grew up Jewish and joyous in North-West London. In his last month at University, God wooed him into his kingdom and he went on to work for ten years in advertising – a fact he is still prepared to admit. Gripped by a desire to dig into God's word, he took a career break to study at the London School of Theology. The career break turned into a career change and he ended up on the staff teaching Communications, and Engaging with Contemporary Culture, and serving as Vice Principal.

He joined the London Institute for Contemporary Christianity in 1999, eager to focus on the call to see all God's people empowered to live their whole lives – Monday to Saturday, as well as Sunday – in dynamic and fruitful relationship with Christ. His books include *Adventure, Thank God it's Monday*, and *Fruitfulness on the Frontline*. He's married to Katriina, a Finn, and they have three splendidly different children. Mark enjoys films and fiction (a lot), and does a passable imitation of Mr Bean and a terrible one of Sean Connery. His wife wishes it were the other way round. His children wish he wouldn't do either.

Muddy
Pearl

If you enjoyed reading this, please tell a friend.
Send us a review, any errors you find, thoughts, comments
or chocolate to *books@muddypearl.com* .

We think you might like these other books by Mark Greene,
also available from Muddy Pearl:

Adventure
Thank God it's Monday

From the Muddy Pearl Team
Stephanie, Anna, Fiona, Healey and Josh
muddypearl.com